This Book belongs to:

..................................................................

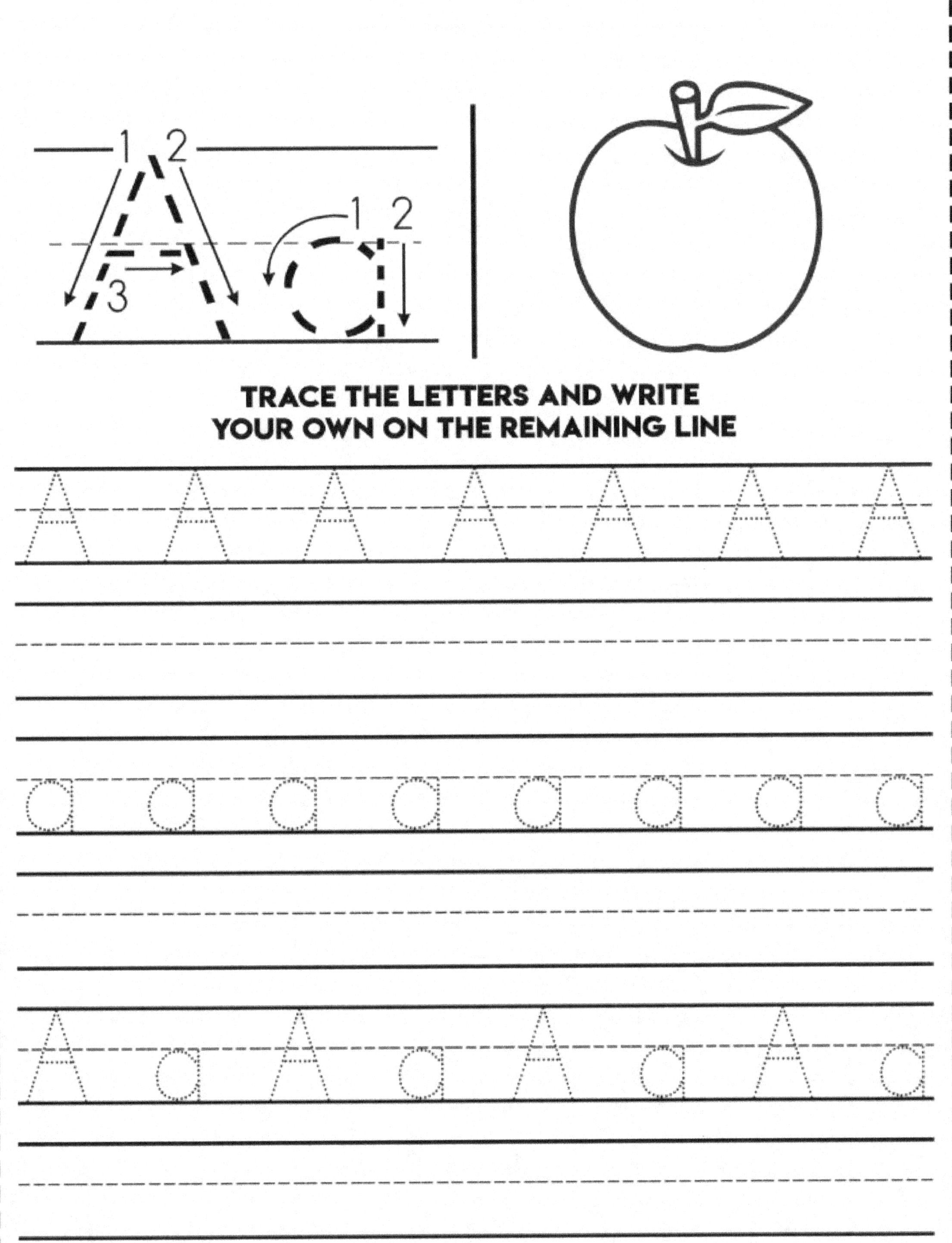
TRACE THE LETTERS AND WRITE
YOUR OWN ON THE REMAINING LINE

A A A A A A A

A A A A A A A

A A A A A A A

A A A A A A A

A A A A A A A

A A A A A A A

a a a a a a a

a a a a a a a

a a a a a a a

a a a a a a a

a a a a a a a

These Words begin with the Letter **A**. Trace each Word, and then print Word on the Line.

apple

and

amaze

area

alligator

ant

astronaut

aunt

ask

1  2
1
3
2
Trace the letters and write your own on the remaining line.

b b b b b b b

b b b b b b b

b b b b b b b

b b b b b b b

b b b b b b b

b b b b b b b

These Words begin with the Letter **B**. Trace each Word, and then print Word on the Line.

butterfly

banana

bee

big

bye

body

boa

bake

but

Trace the letters and write your own on the remaining line.

c c c c c c c

c c c c c c c

c c c c c c c

c c c c c c c

c c c c c c c

c c c c c c c

c c c c c c c

c c c c c c c

c c c c c c c

c c c c c c c

c c c c c c c

c c c c c c c

These Words begin with the Letter **C**. Trace each Word, and then print
Word on the Line.

can

cat

cod

cow

cut

camp

card

cabin

clock

Trace the letters and write your own on the remaining line.

d d d d d d d

d d d d d d d

d d d d d d d

d d d d d d d

d d d d d d d

These Words begin with the Letter **D**. Trace each Word, and then print Word on the Line.

dad

dog

do

den

deep

dear

dish

drink

dash

✏️ Trace the letters and write your own on the remaining line.

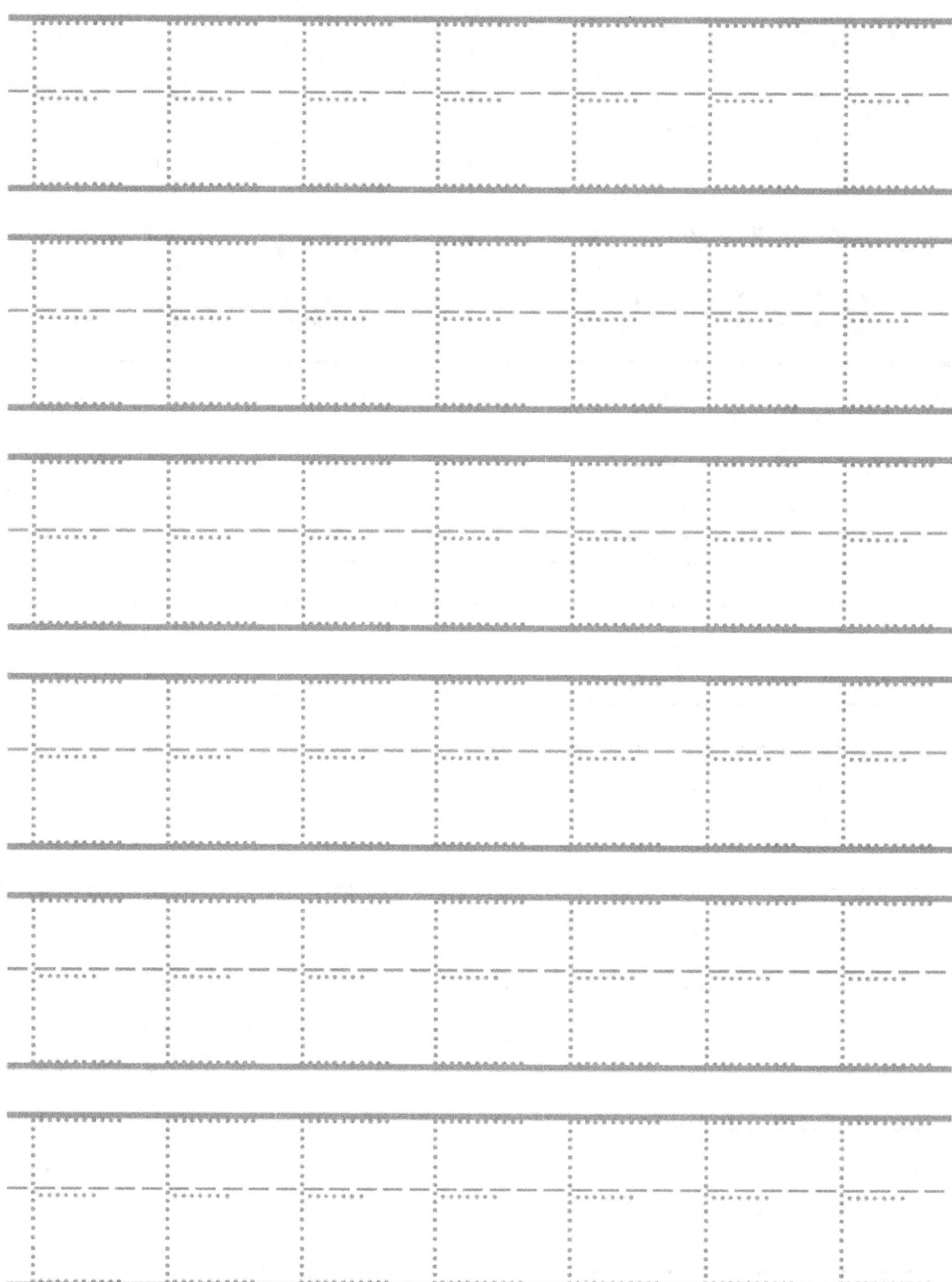

e e e e e e e

e e e e e e e

e e e e e e e

e e e e e e e

e e e e e e e

e e e e e e e

These Words begin with the Letter **E**. Trace each Word, and then print
Word on the Line.

elefant

ear

eat

egg

elf

end

eye

else

enter

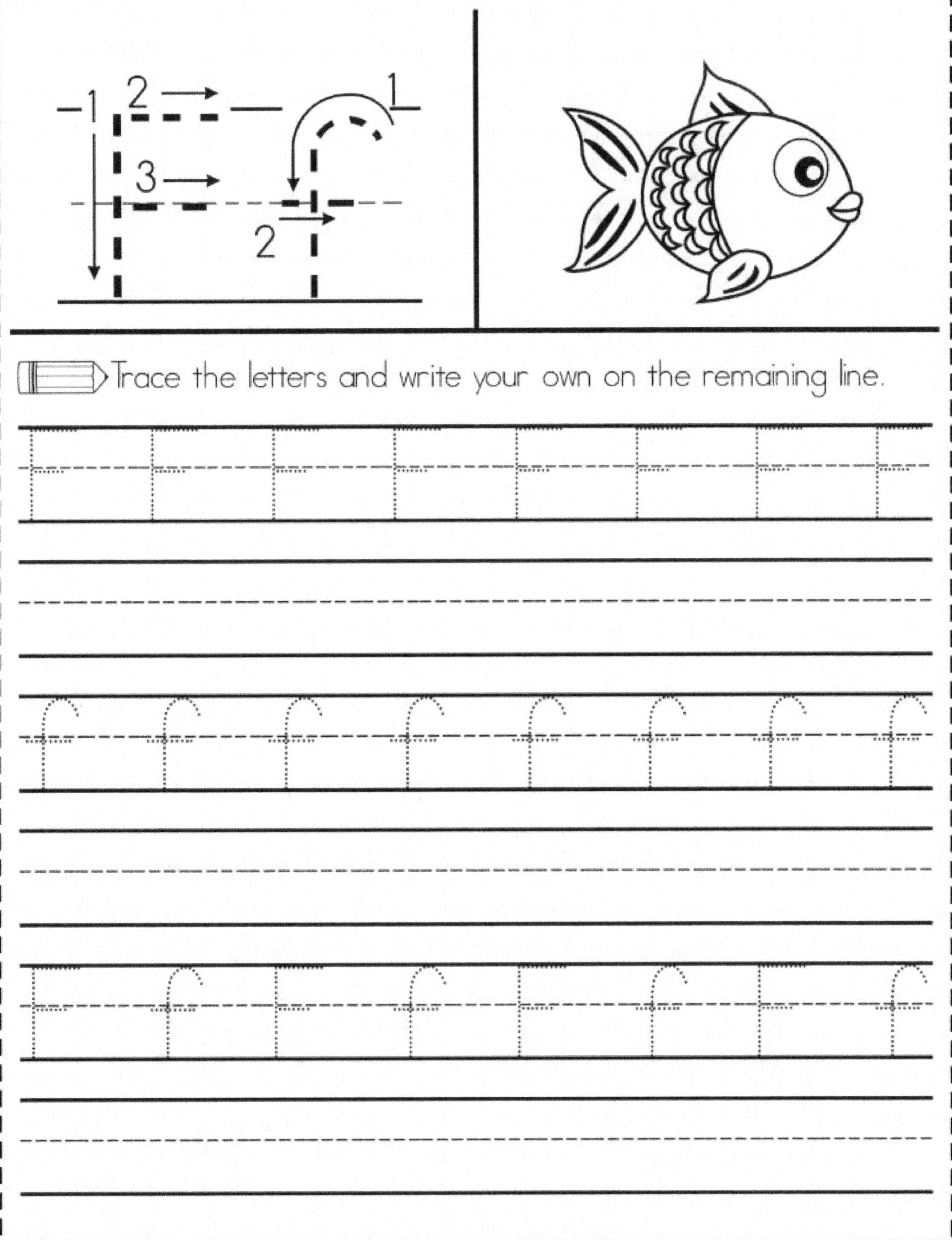


Trace the letters and write your own on the remaining line.

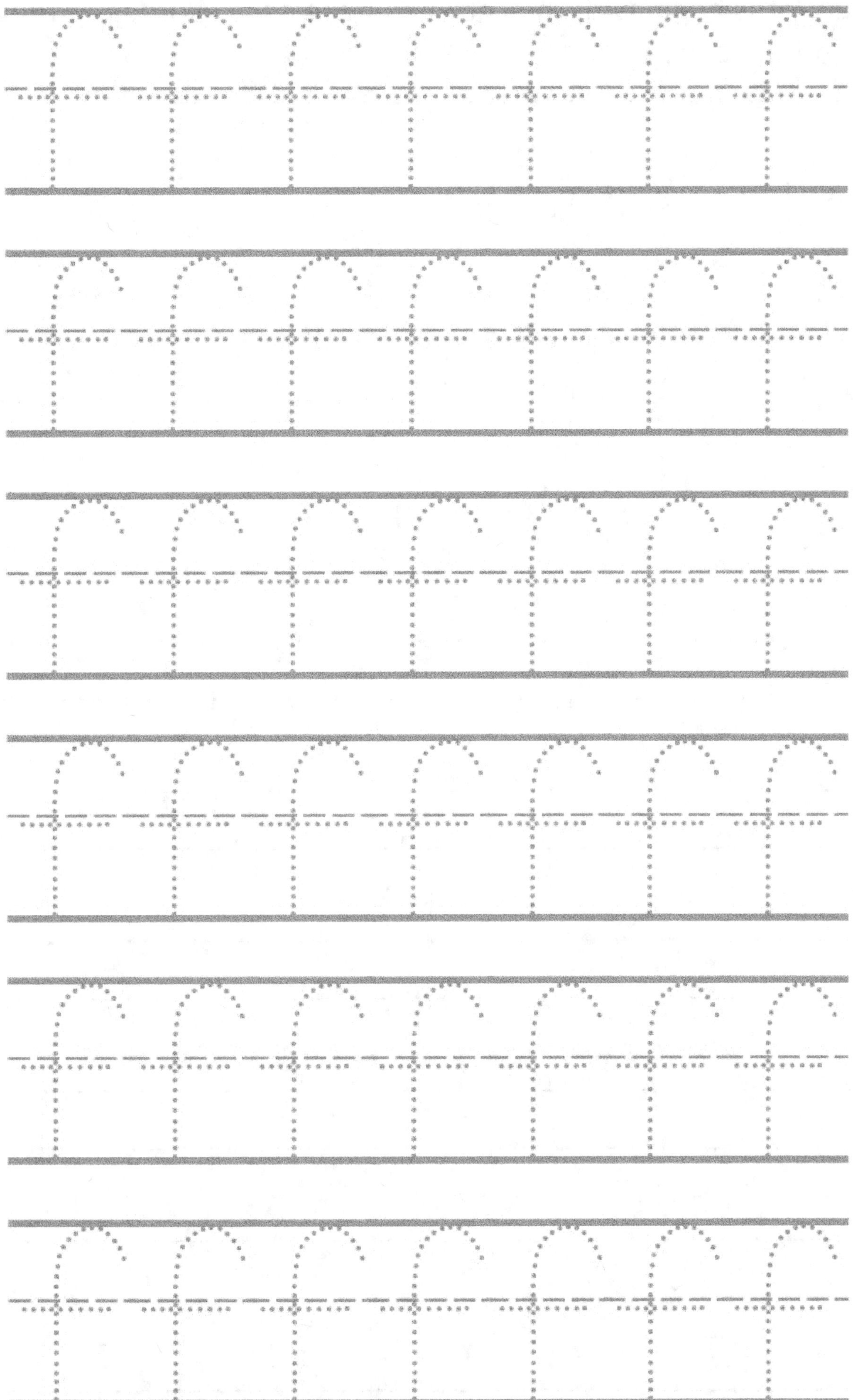

These Words begin with the Letter **F**. Trace each Word, and then print Word on the Line.

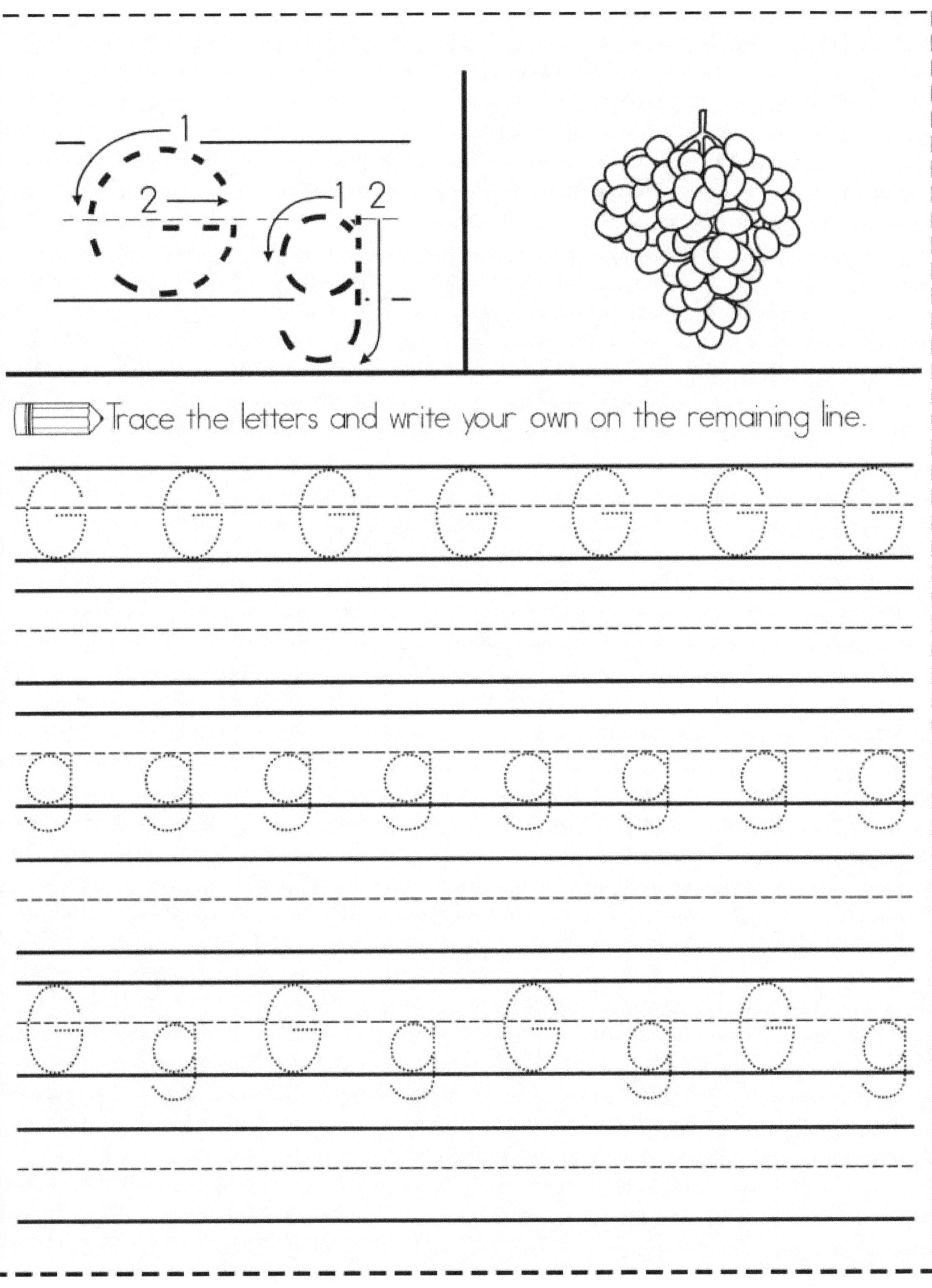

Trace the letters and write your own on the remaining line.

G G G G G G G

G G G G G G G

G G G G G G G

G G G G G G G

G G G G G G G

G G G G G G G

g g g g g g g

g g g g g g g

g g g g g g g

g g g g g g g

g g g g g g g

These Words begin with the Letter **G**. Trace each Word, and then print Word on the Line.

grape

gab

gap

gas

gut

god

good

glass

green

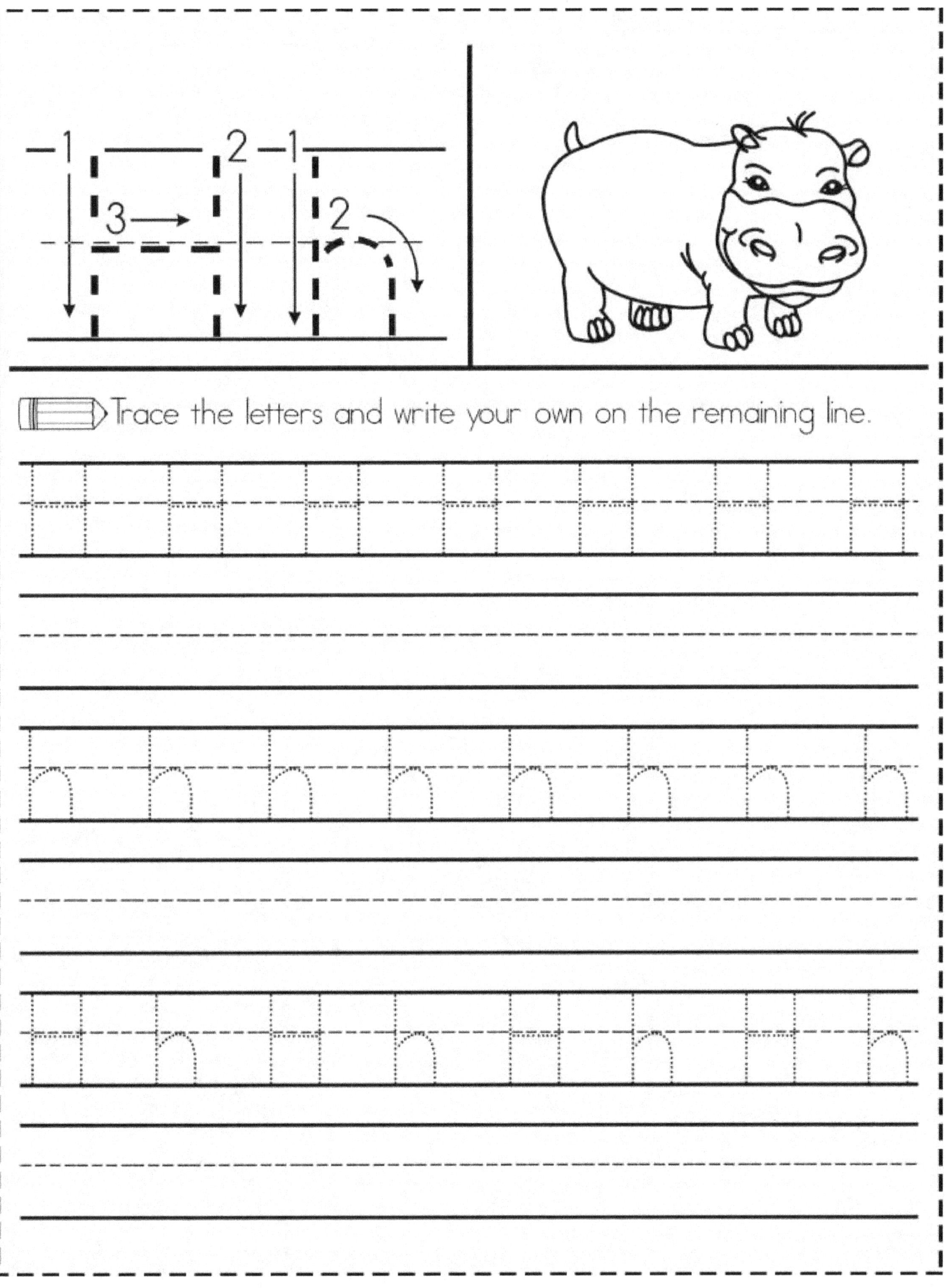



Trace the letters and write your own on the remaining line.

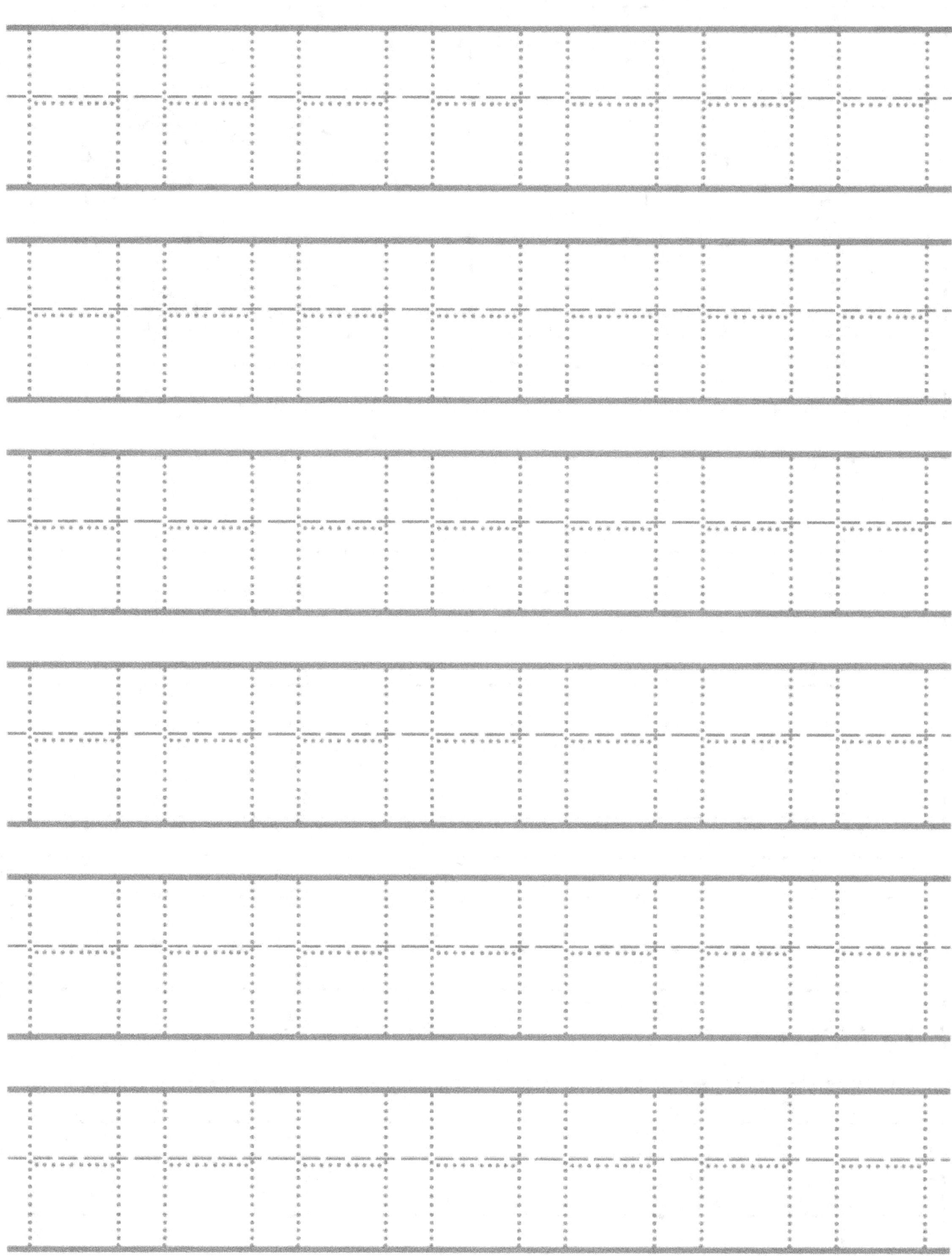

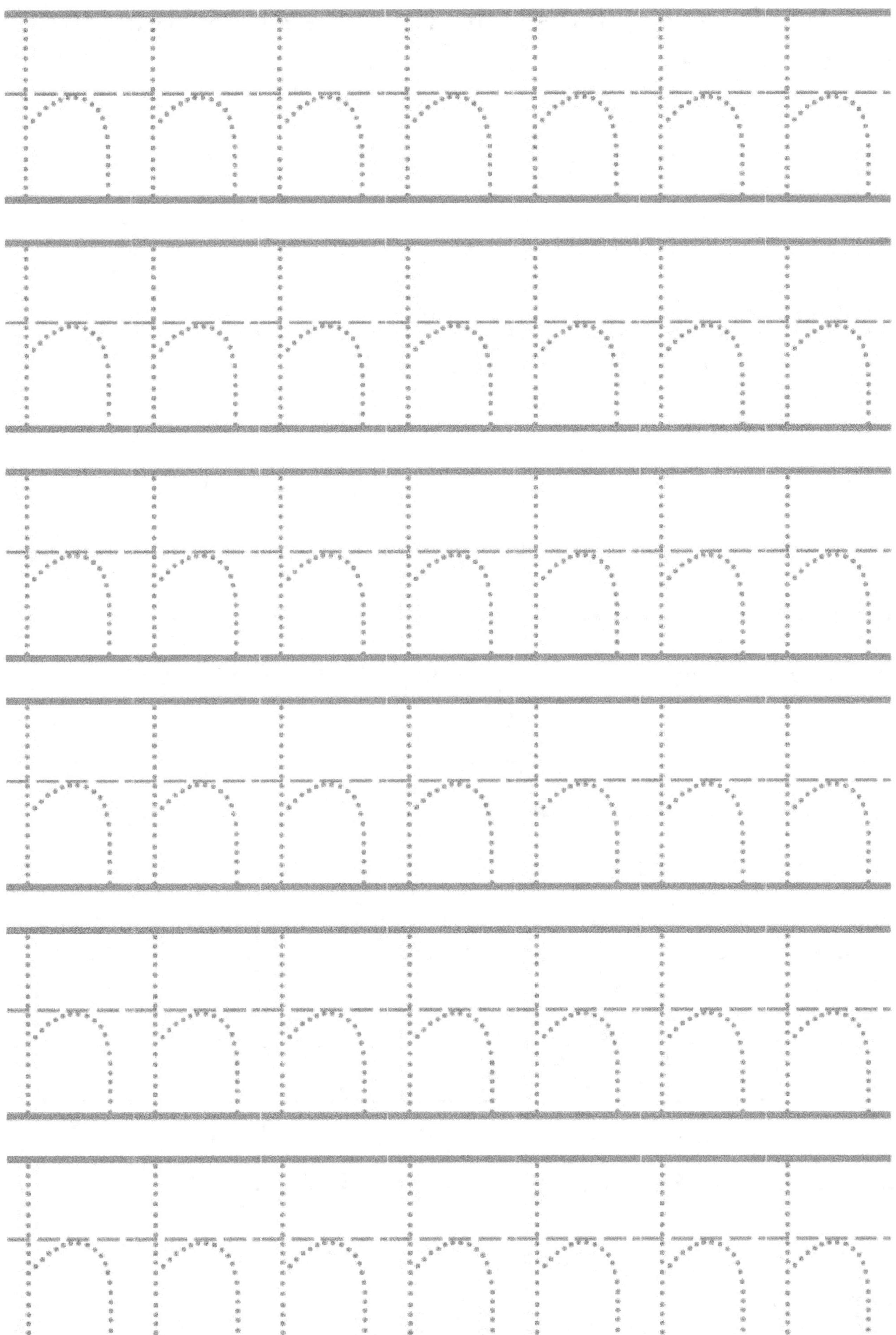

These Words begin with the Letter **H**. Trace each Word, and then print Word on the Line.

hat

hay

hey

hand

his

hold

head

hard

hair

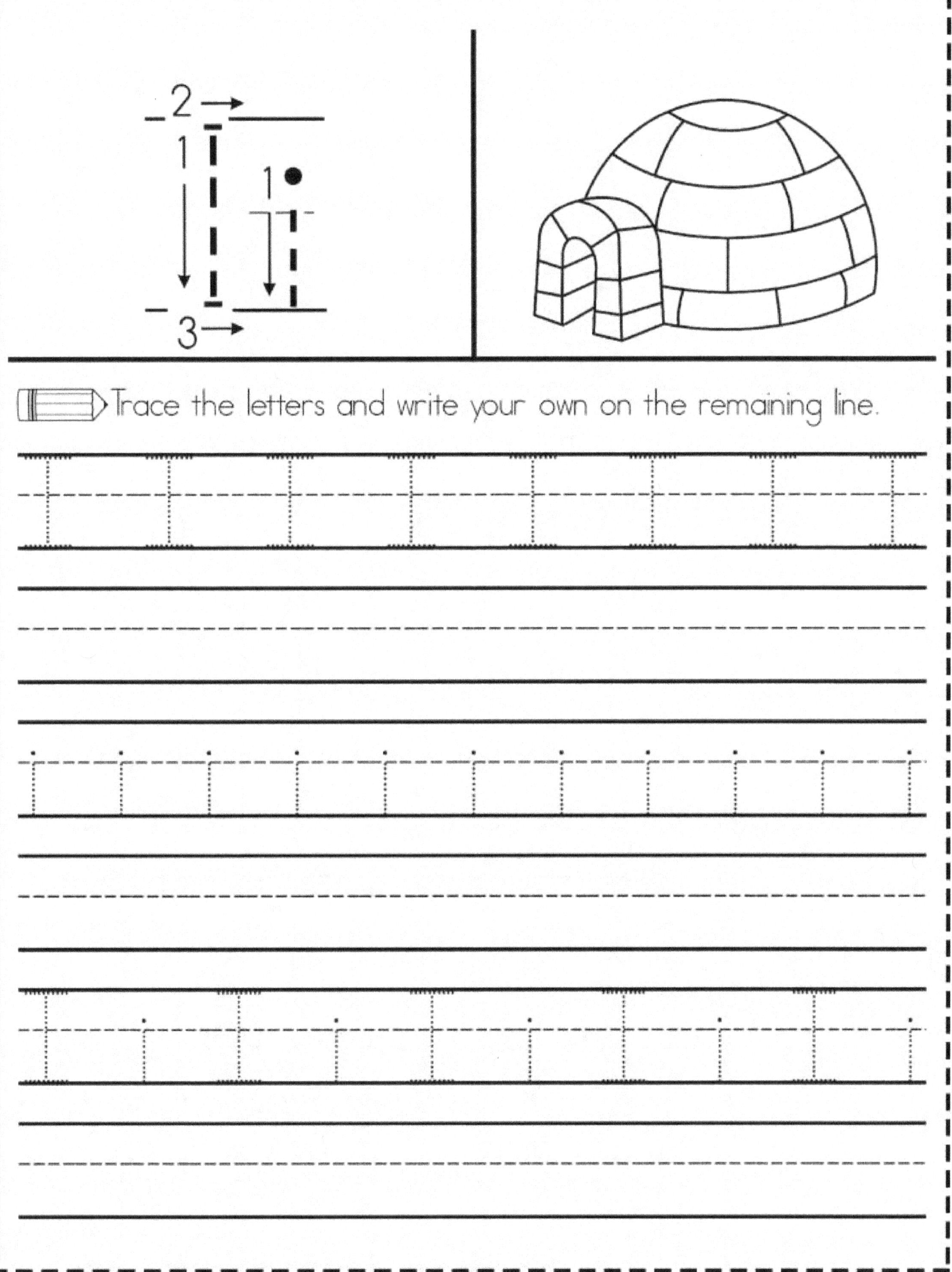


Trace the letters and write your own on the remaining line.

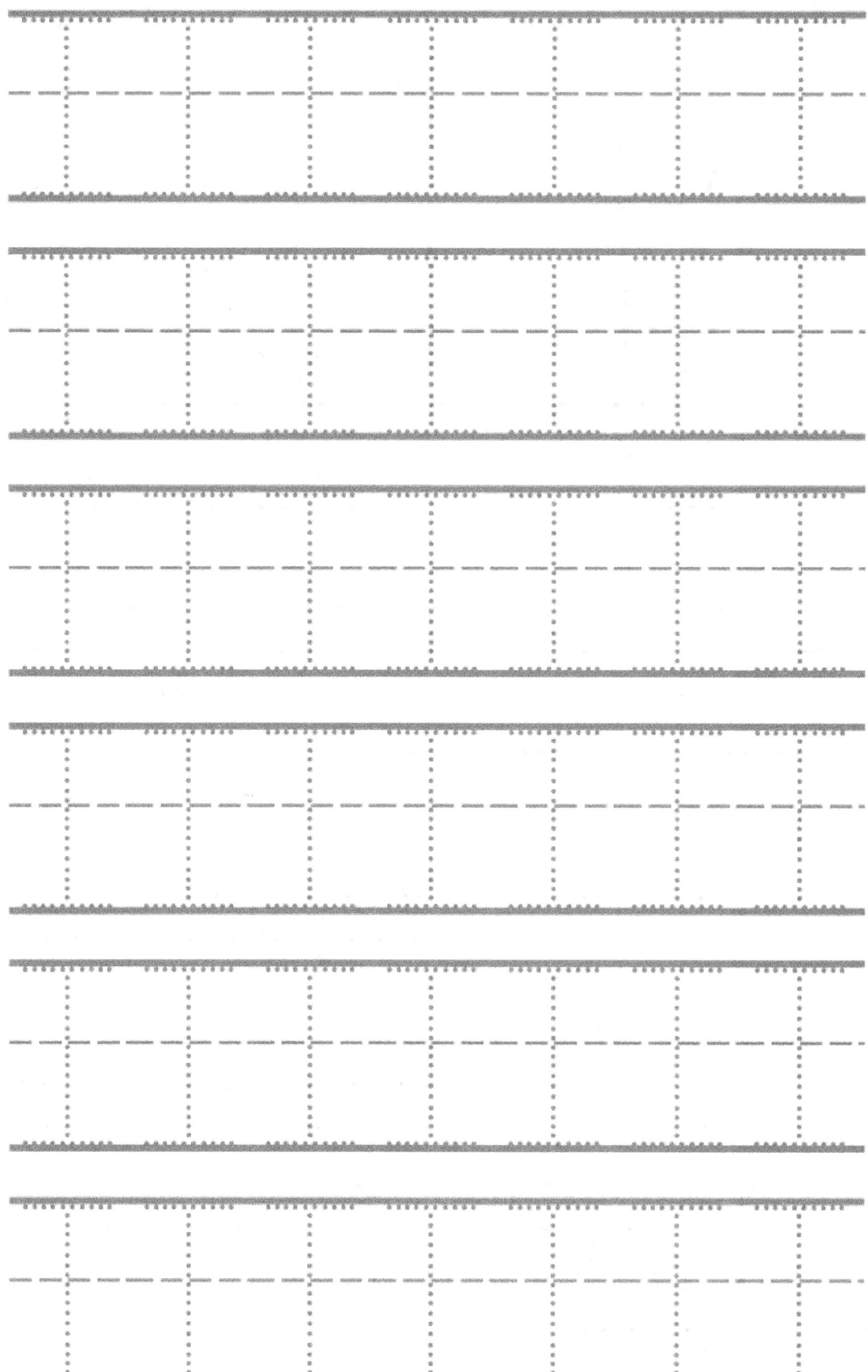

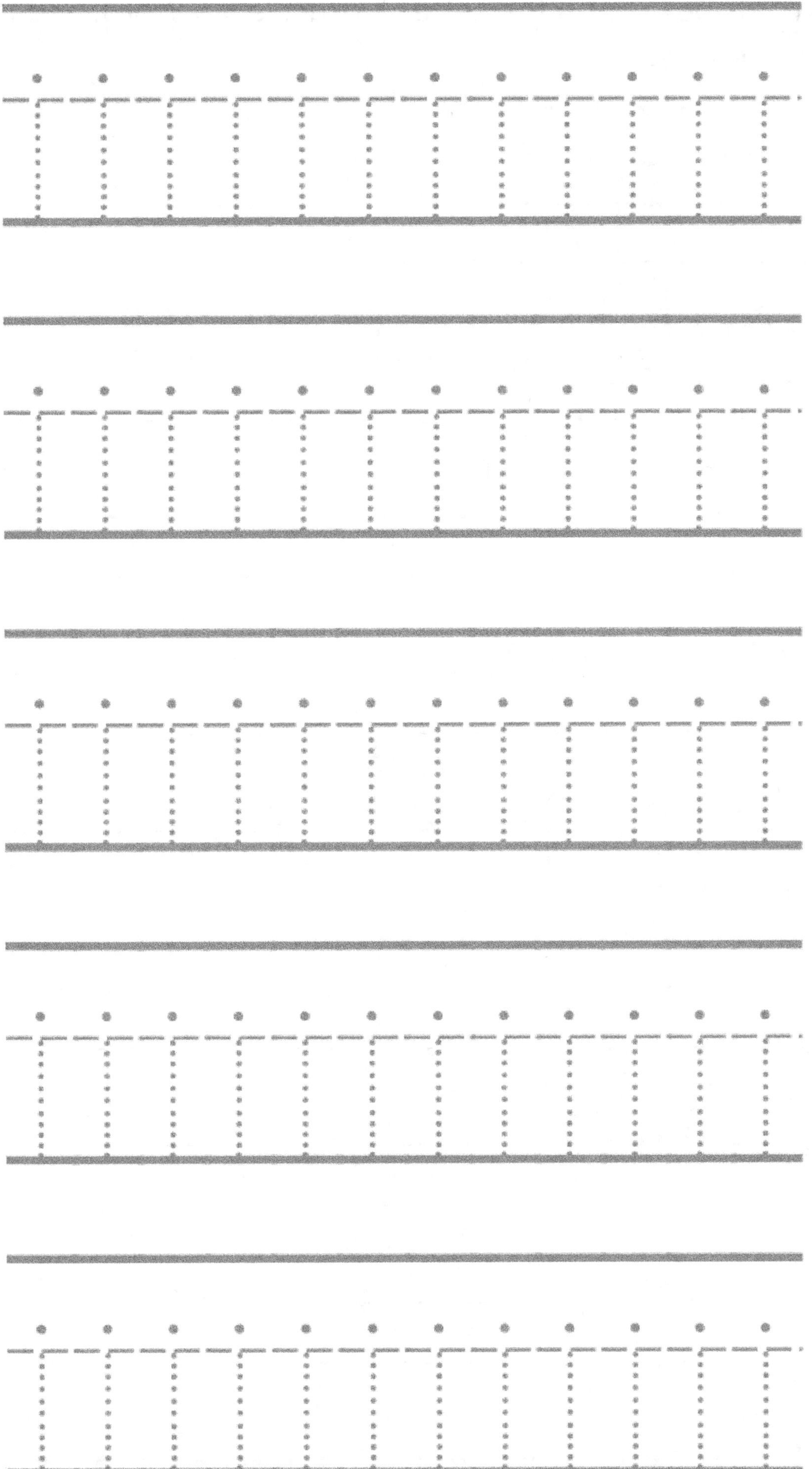

These Words begin with the Letter **I**. Trace each Word, and then print
Word on the Line.

ice

idea

it

into

itself

iron

island

insect

item

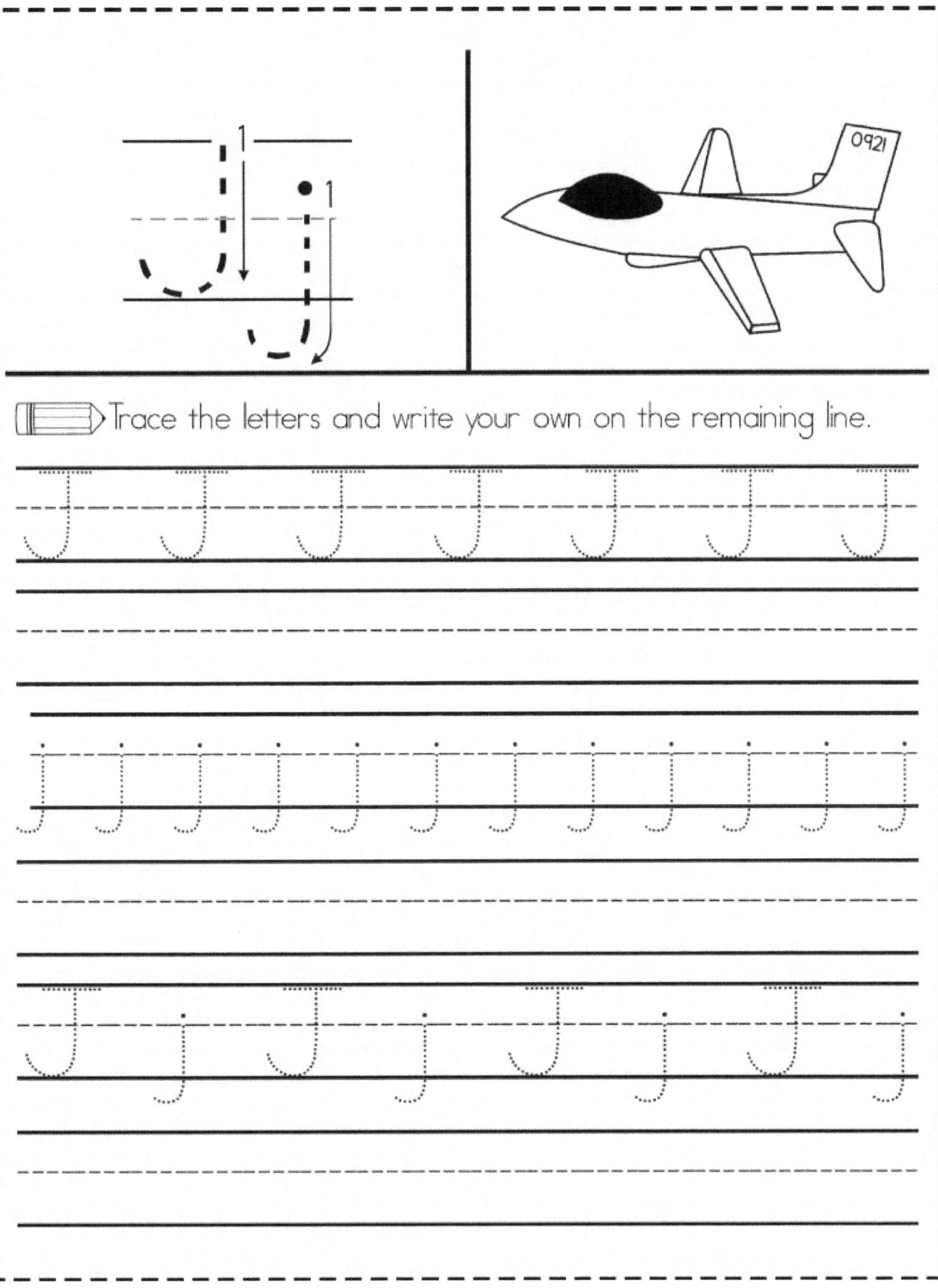

Trace the letters and write your own on the remaining line.

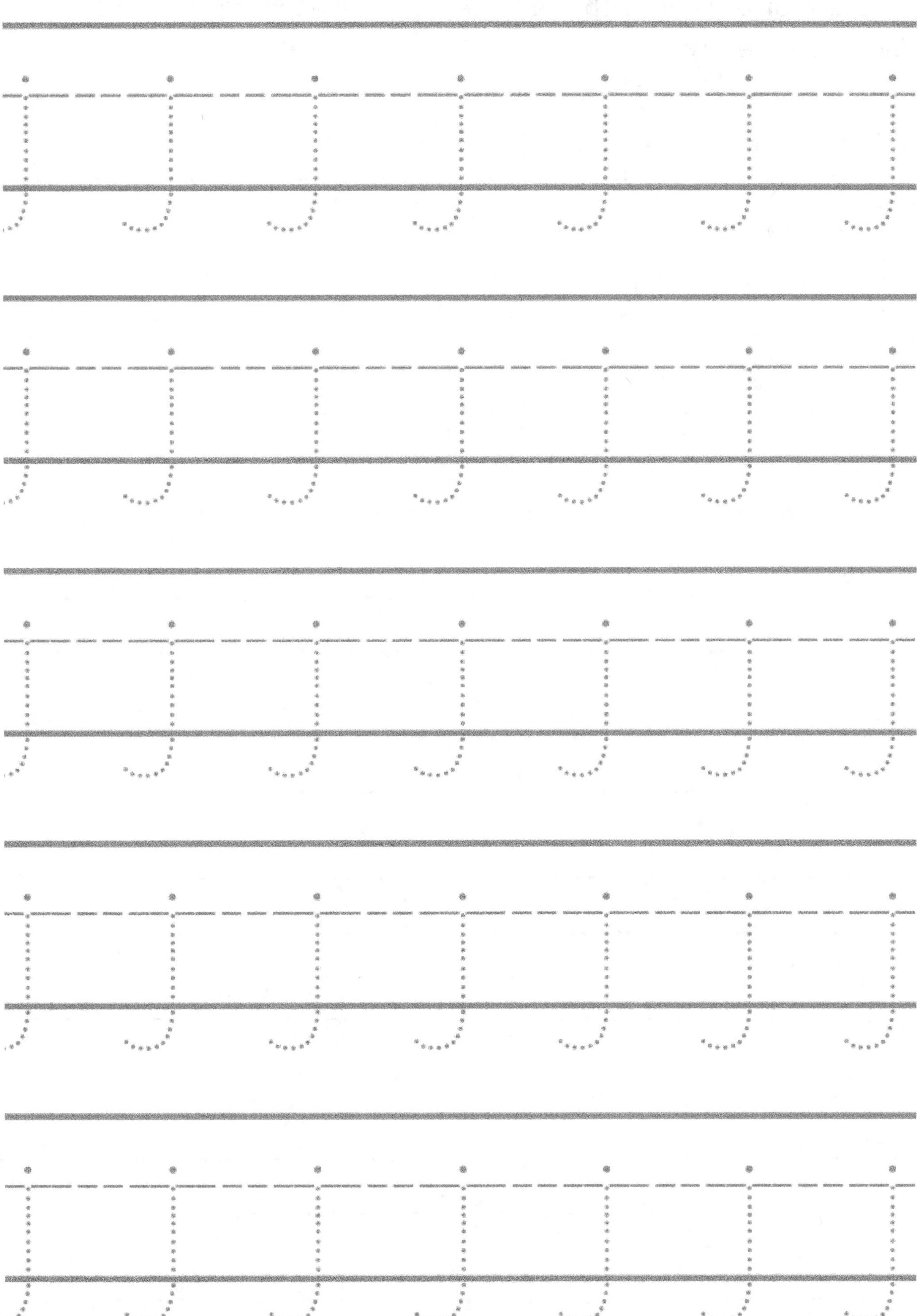

These Words begin with the Letter **J**. Trace each Word, and then print Word on the Line.

Jet

Joy

Jacket

Jog

Jungle

Jewel

Jail

Jingle

Jam

Trace the letters and write your own on the remaining line.

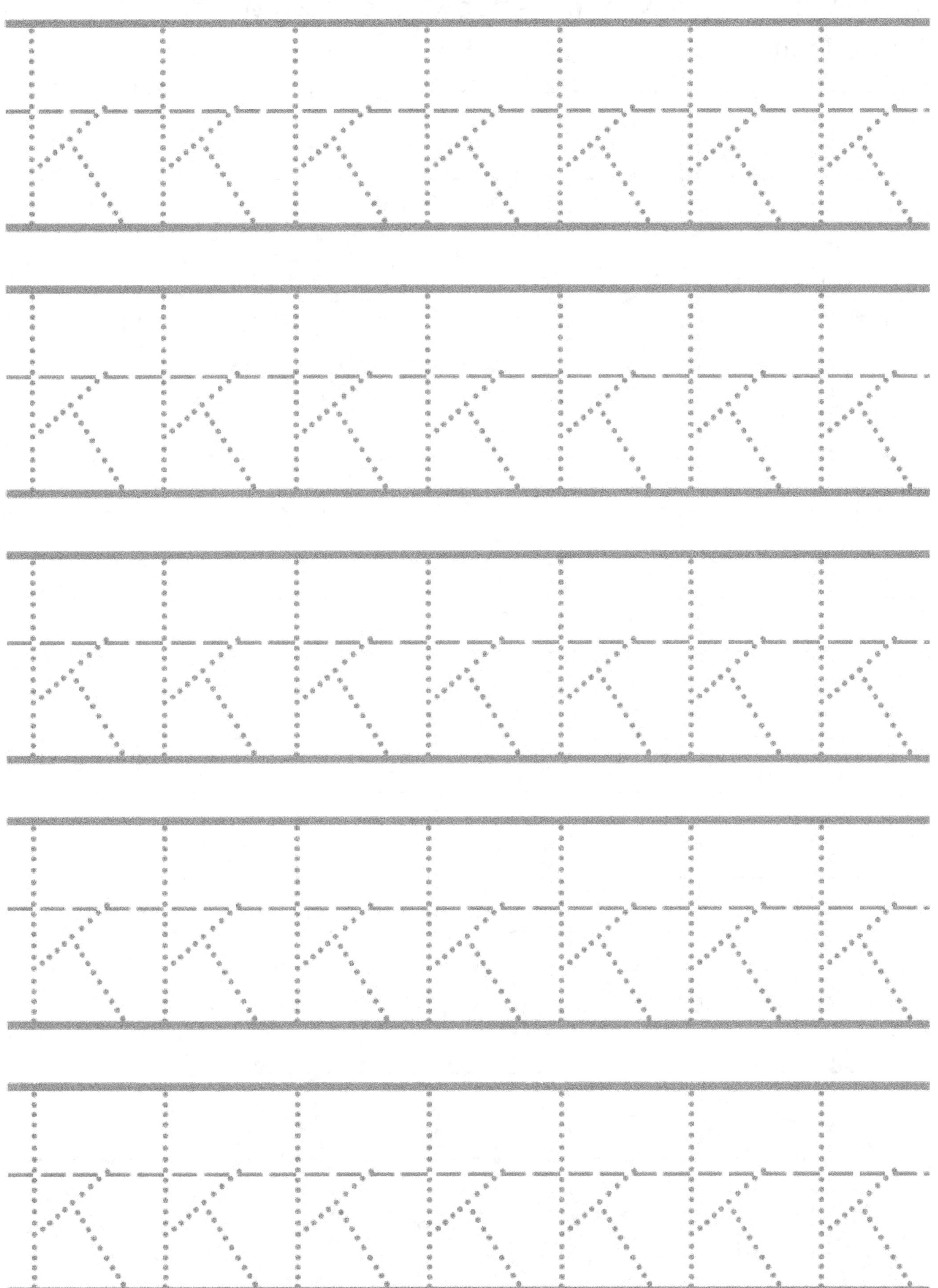

These Words begin with the Letter **K**. Trace each Word, and then print Word on the Line.

key

kite

king

koala

kick

kid

knee

kelp

knot

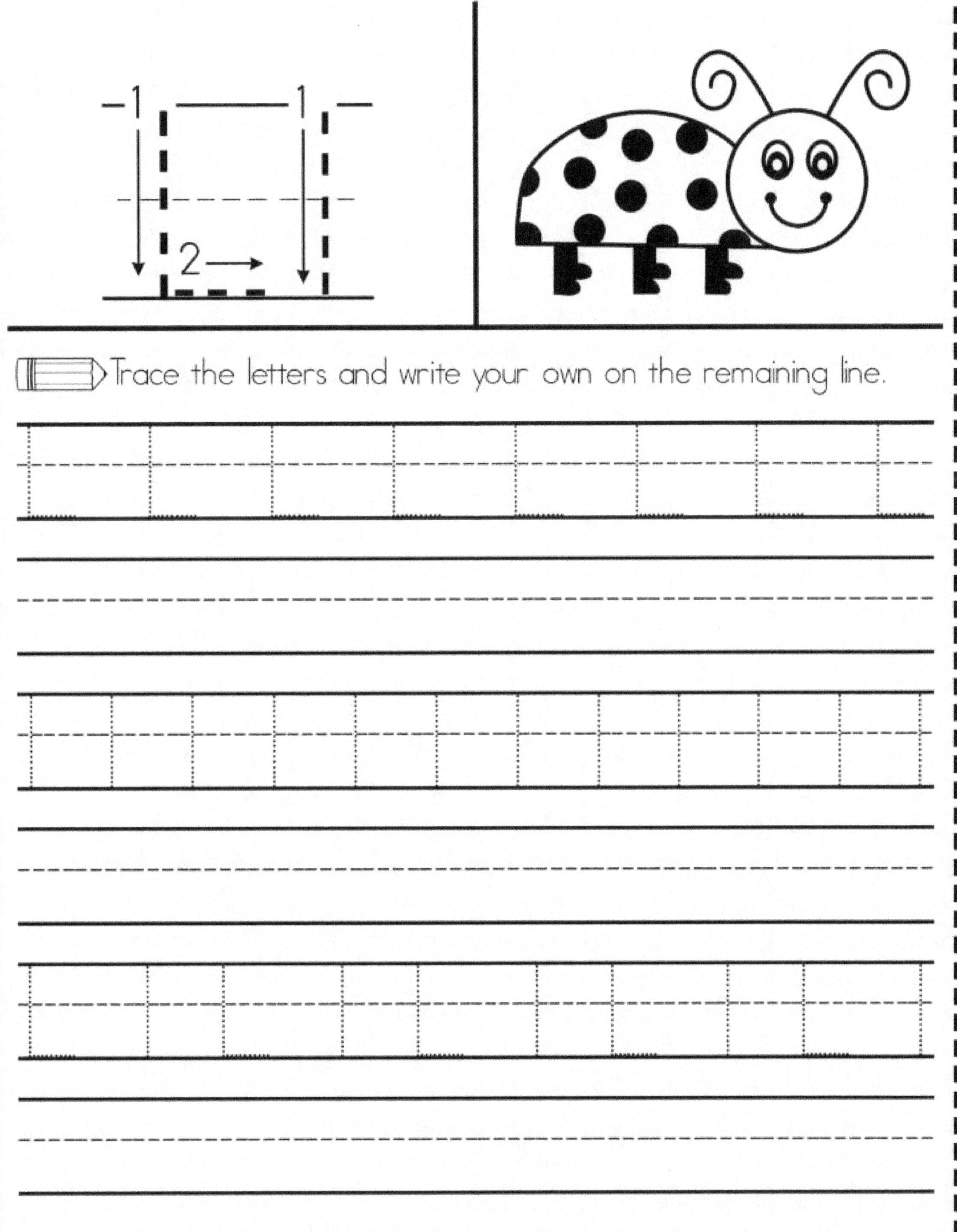



Trace the letters and write your own on the remaining line.

These Words begin with the Letter **L**. Trace each Word, and then print Word on the Line.

lamb

leaf

let

light

lid

line

lion

log

lunch

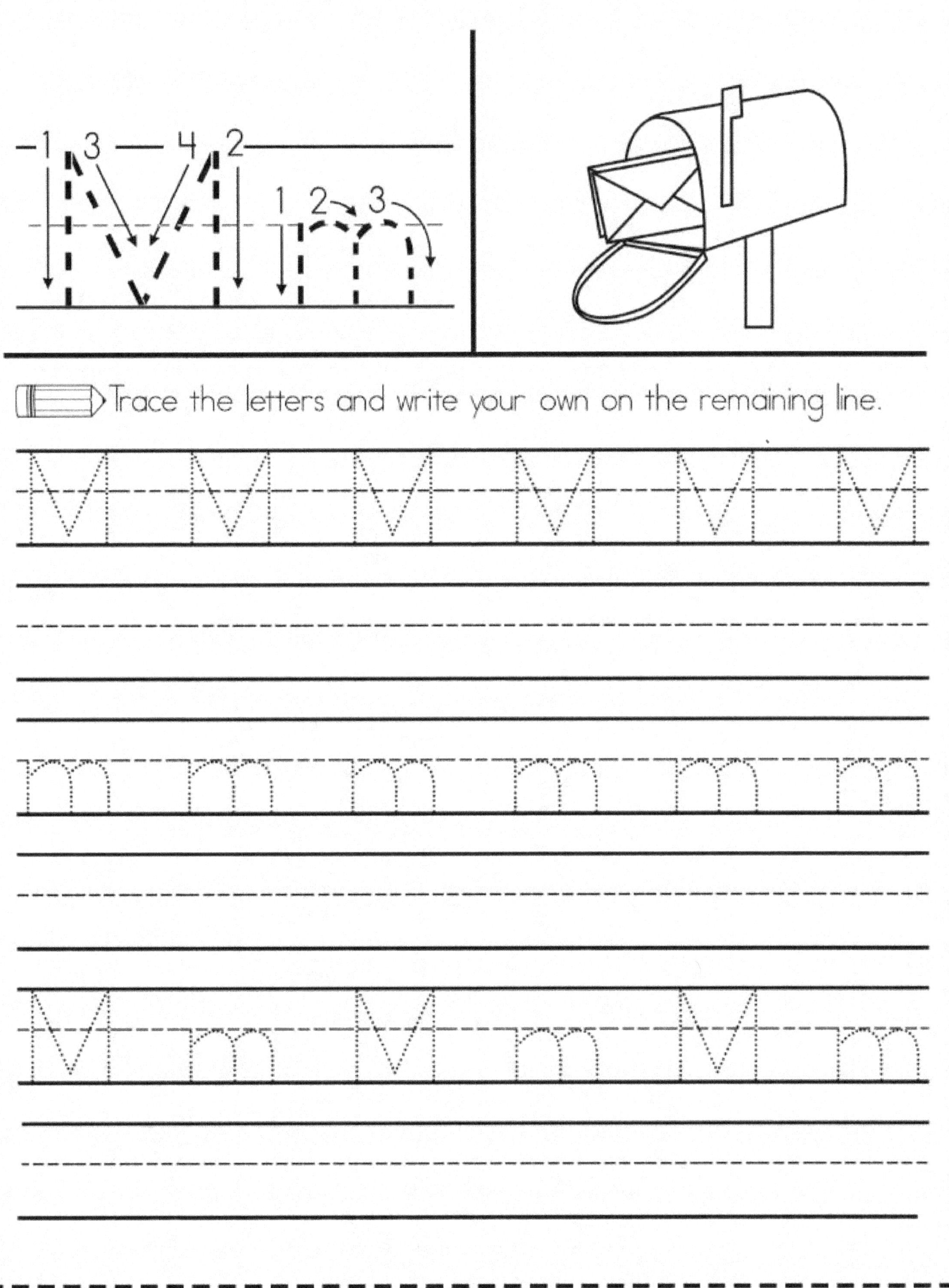



✏️ Trace the letters and write your own on the remaining line.

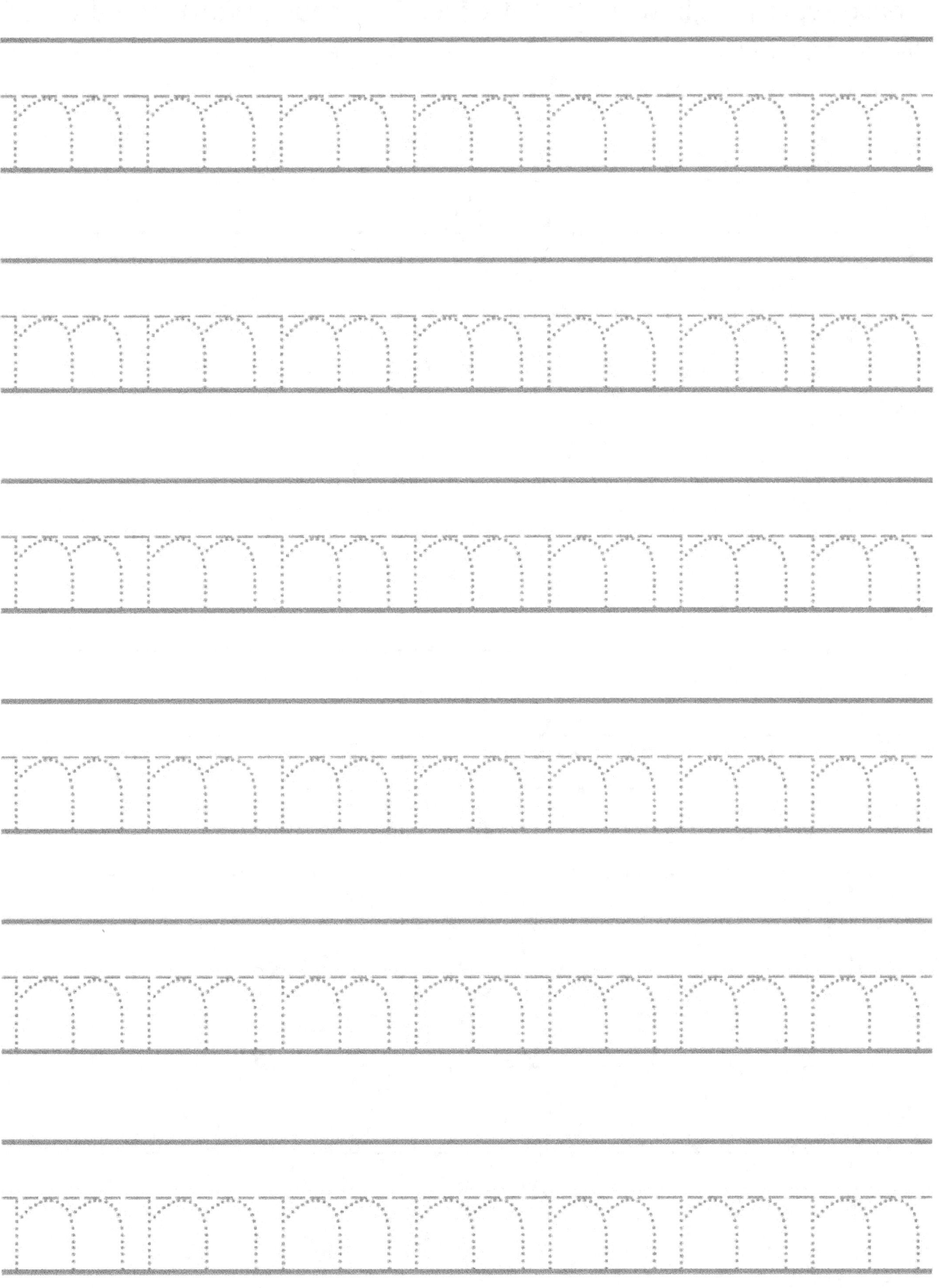

These Words begin with the Letter **M**. Trace each Word, and then print Word on the Line.

Trace the letters and write your own on the remaining line.

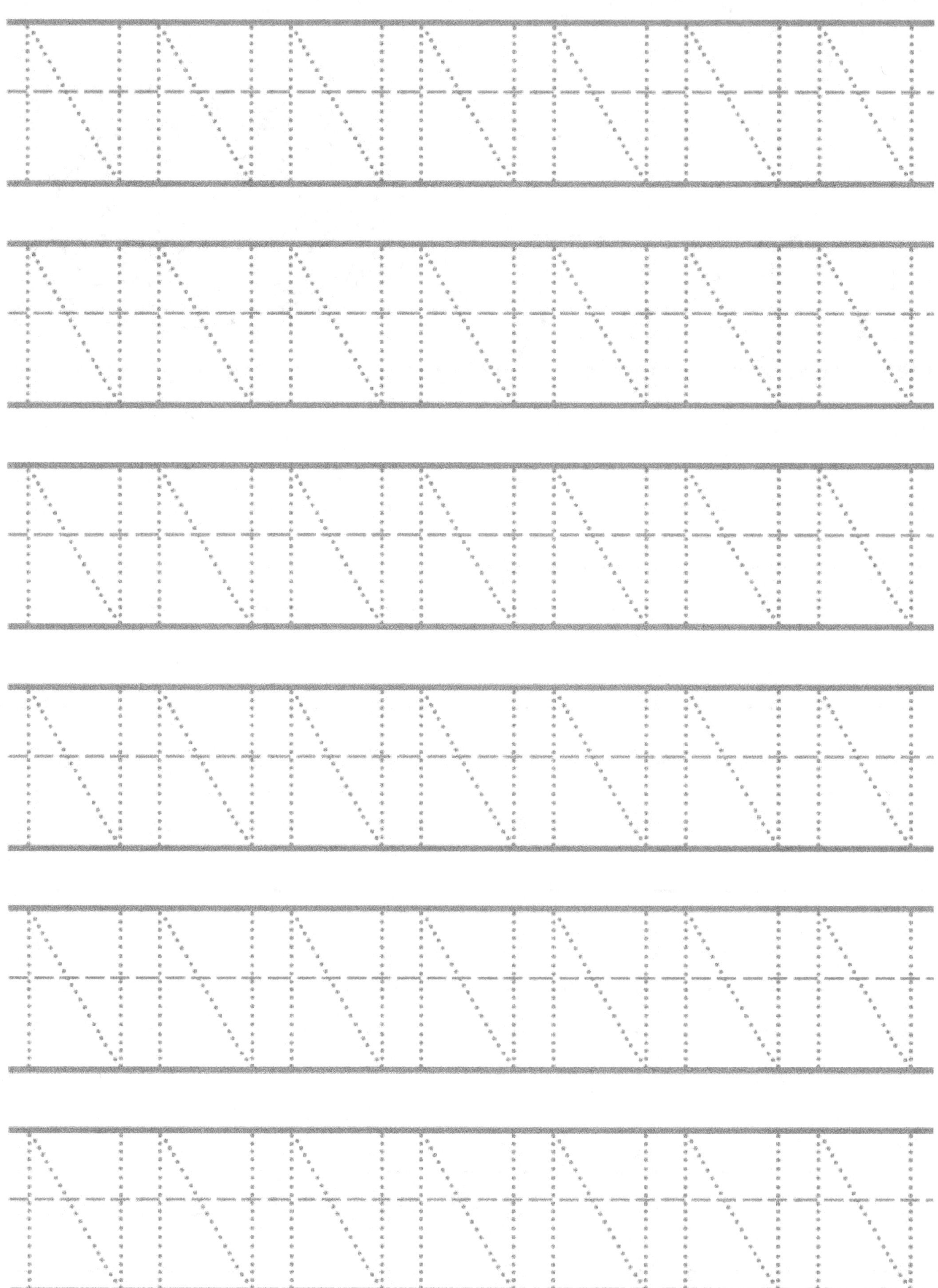

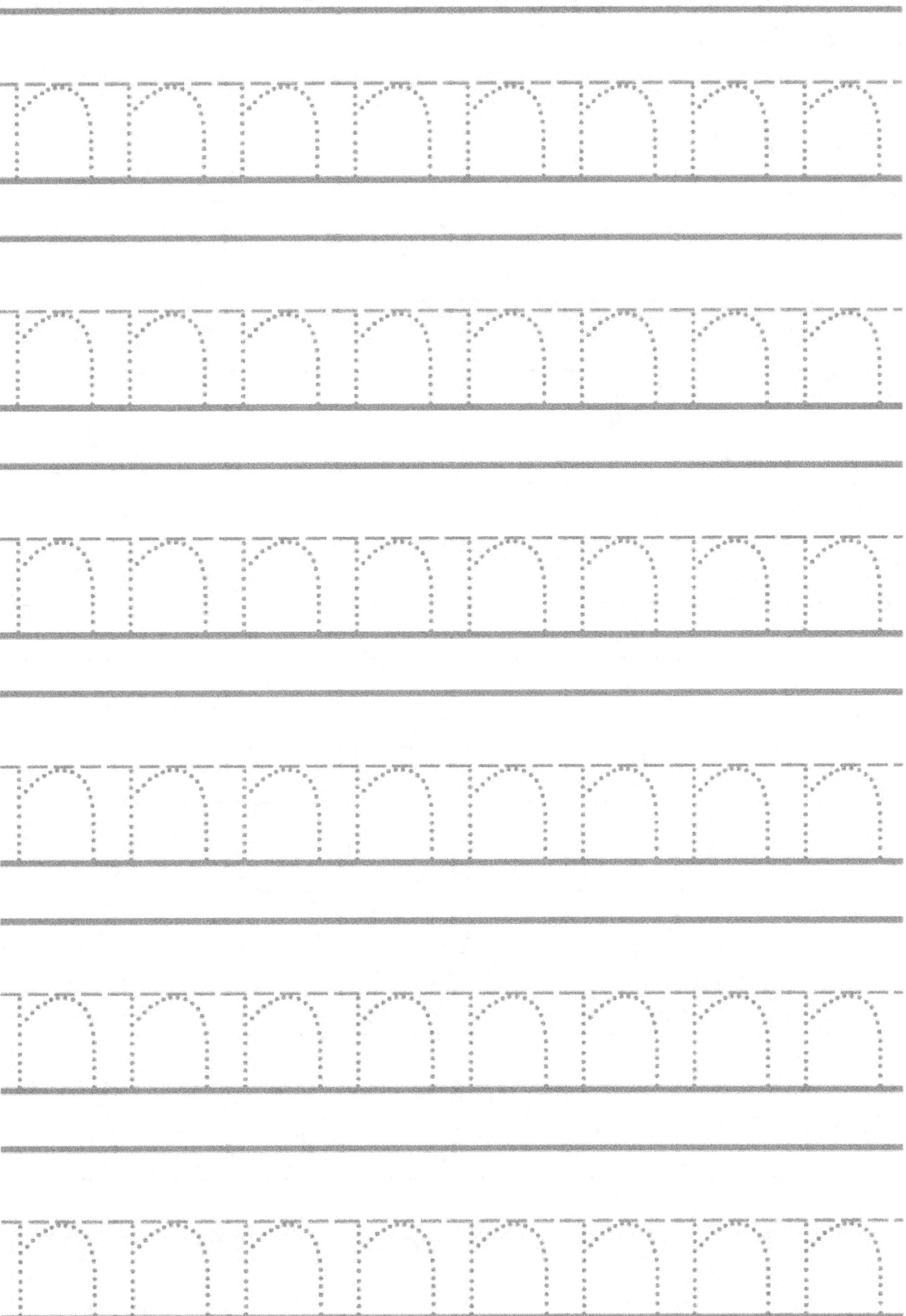

These Words begin with the Letter **N**. Trace each Word, and then print
Word on the Line.

name

nap

near

new

nice

none

number

north

night

1
1
Trace the letters and write your own on the remaining line.

These Words begin with the Letter **O**. Trace each Word, and then print Word on the Line.

off

on

one

our

out

own

oil

over

open

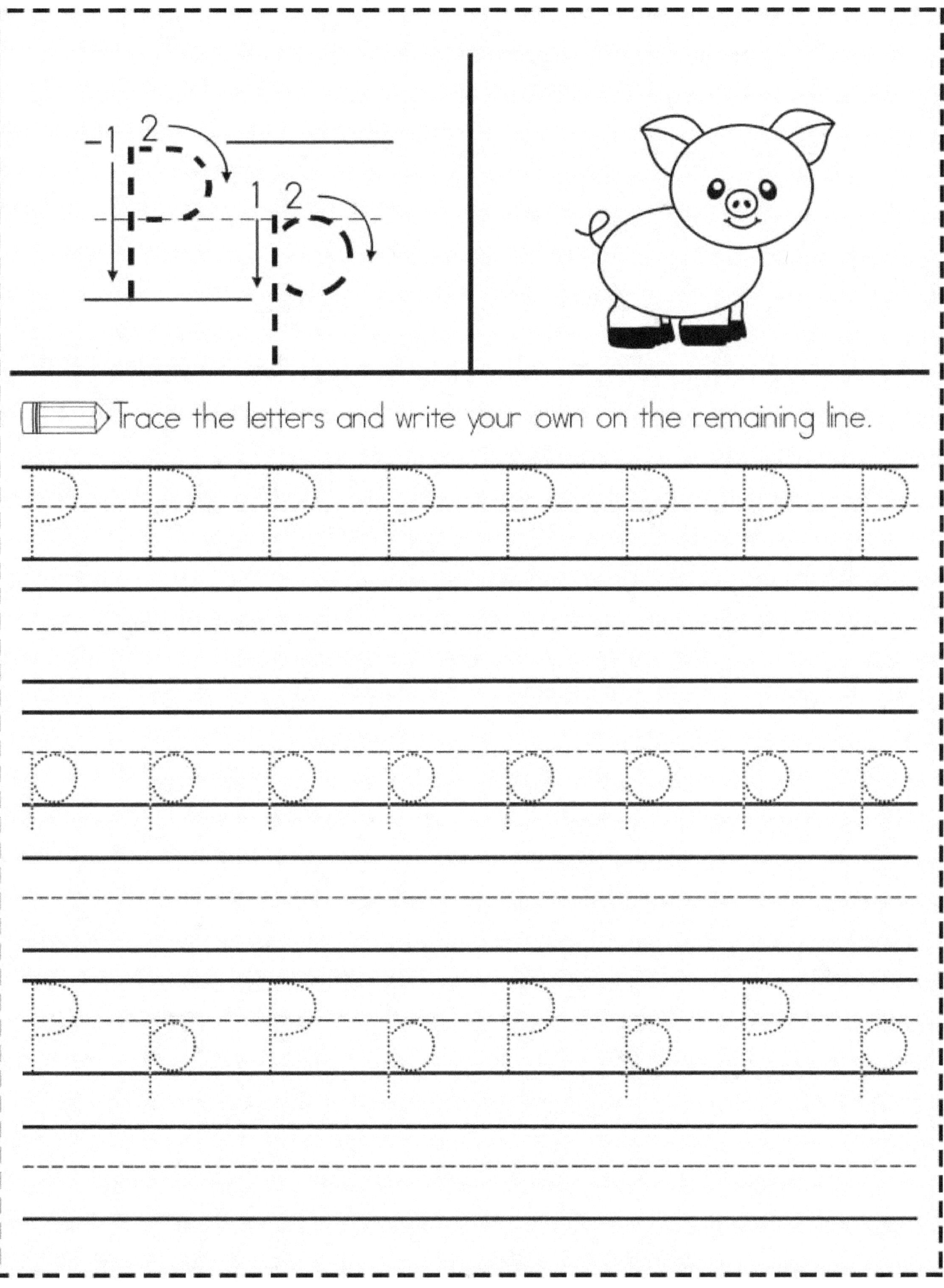


Trace the letters and write your own on the remaining line.

P P P P P P P P

P P P P P P P P

P P P P P P P P

P P P P P P P P

P P P P P P P P

P P P P P P P P

P P P P P P P P

P P P P P P P P

p p p p p p p

p p p p p p p

p p p p p p p

p p p p p p p

p p p p p p p

p p p p p p p

p p p p p p p

These Words begin with the Letter **P**. Trace each Word, and then print
Word on the Line.

paw

pet

play

point

pair

pen

pack

pit

paint

Trace the letters and write your own on the remaining line.

a a a a a a a a a

a a a a a a a a a

a a a a a a a a a

a a a a a a a a a

a a a a a a a a a

a a a a a a a a a

These Words begin with the Letter **Q**. Trace each Word, and then print Word on the Line.

quick

queen

question

quickie

quality

quantity

quack

quarter

quiz

1 2
1 2
3
Trace the letters and write your own on the remaining line.
R R R R R R R R
r r r r r r r r
R r R r R r R r

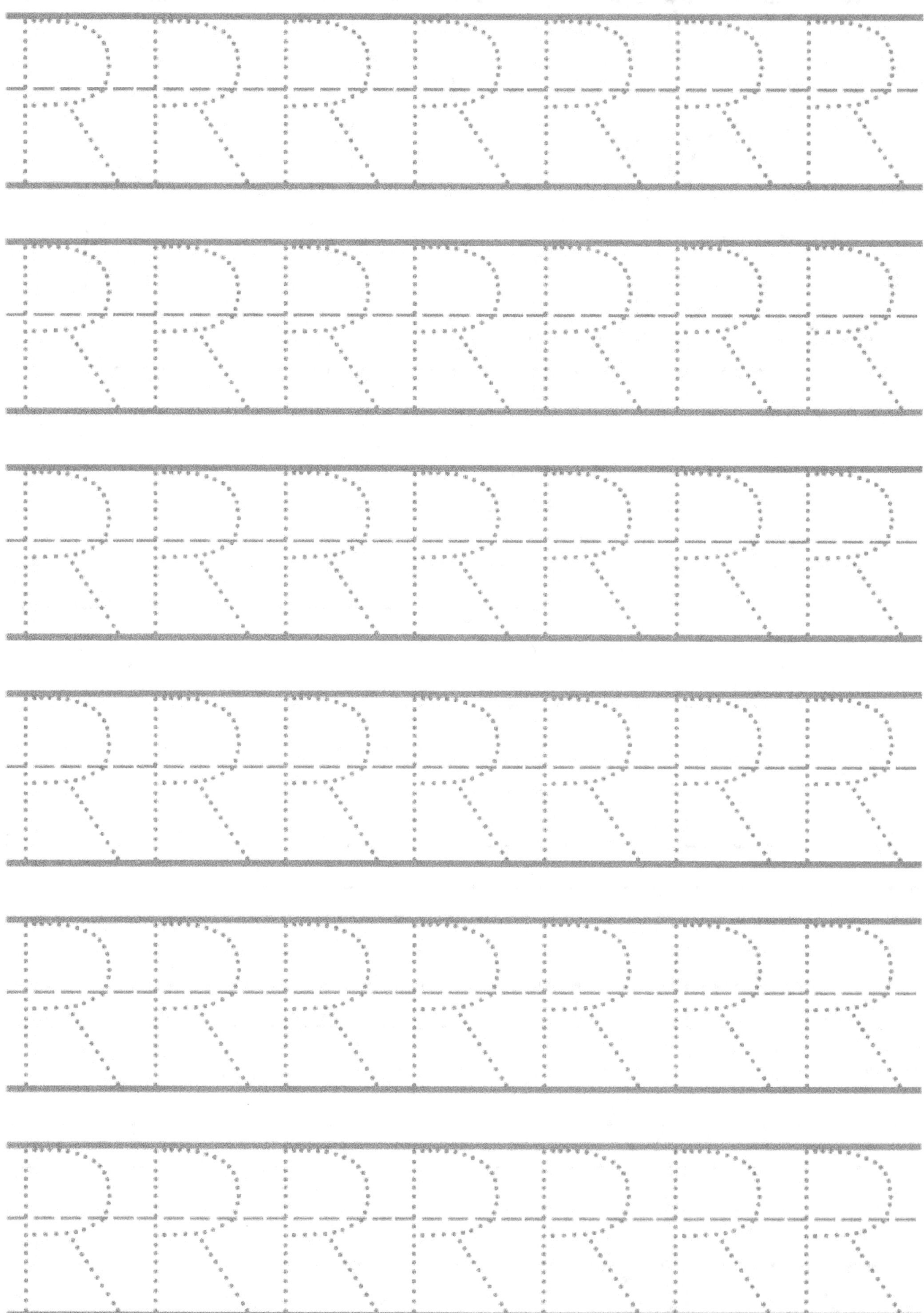

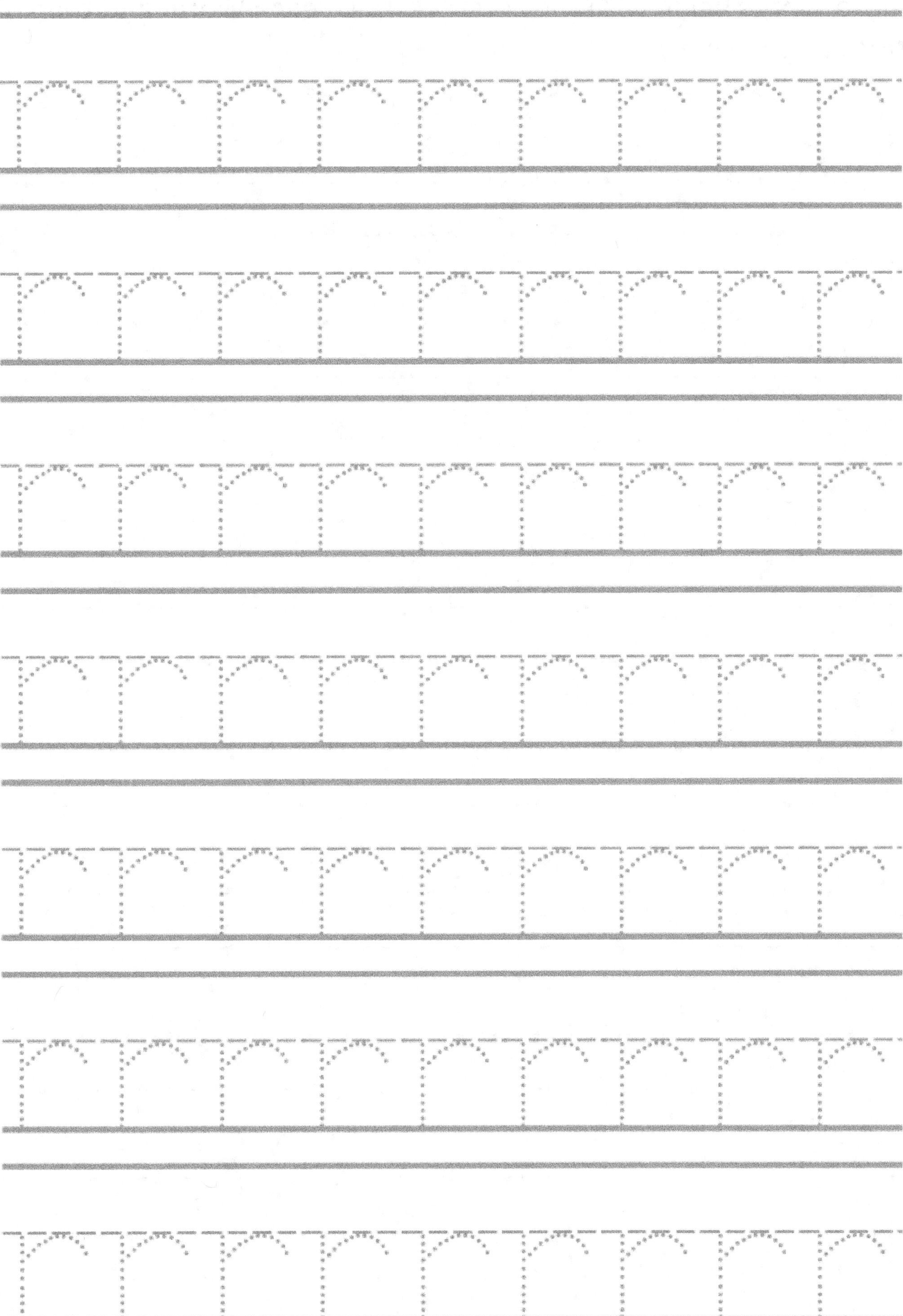

These Words begin with the Letter **R**. Trace each Word, and then print
Word on the Line.

race

rain

red

rest

rich

roll

room

run

root

Trace the letters and write your own on the remaining line.

S S S S S S S S S

S S S S S S S S S

S S S S S S S S S

S S S S S S S S S

S S S S S S S S S

S S S S S S S S S

These Words begin with the Letter **S**. Trace each Word, and then print Word on the Line.

son

sun

say

see

soap

sea

sow

sip

seat

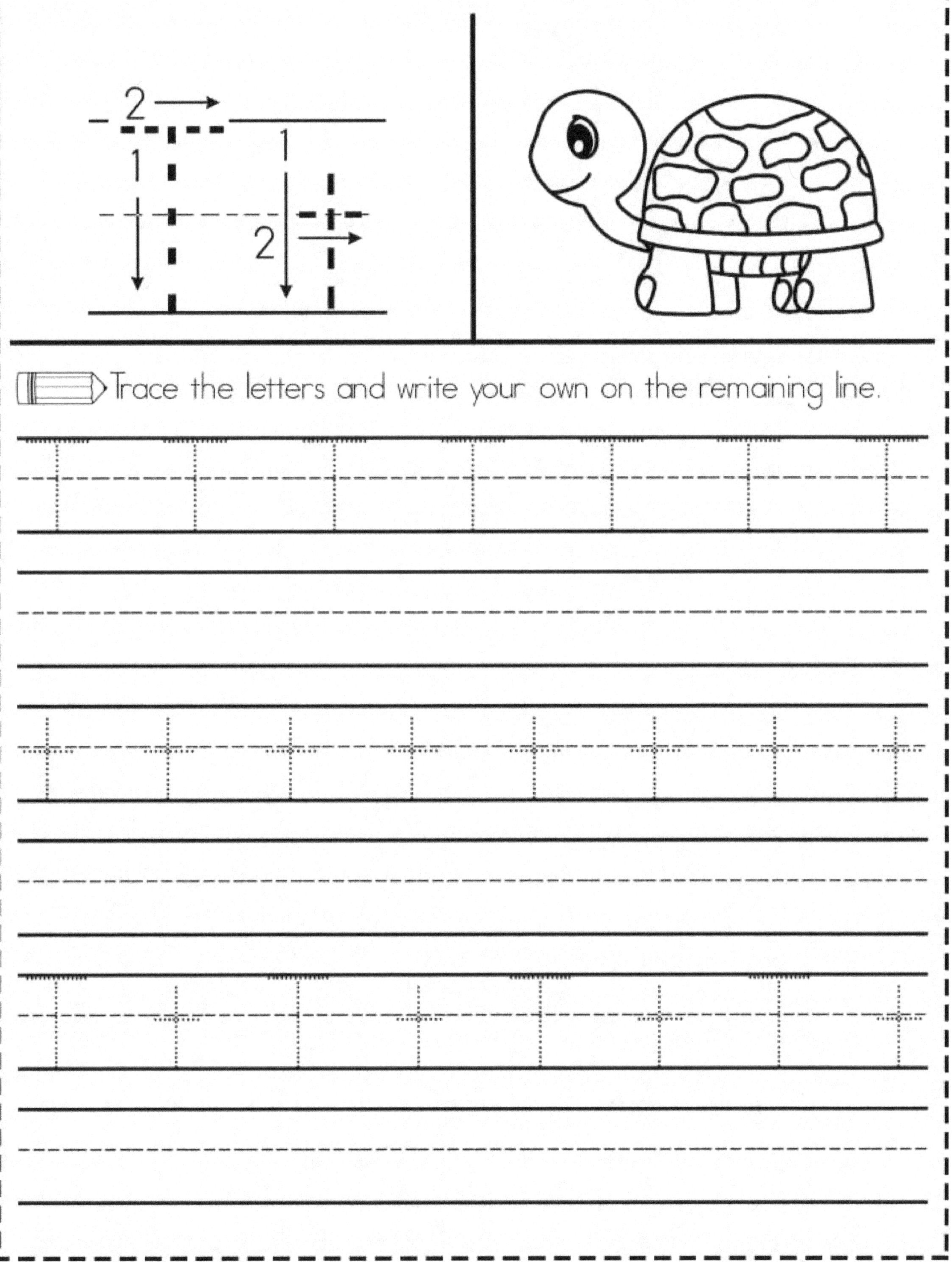



✏️ Trace the letters and write your own on the remaining line.

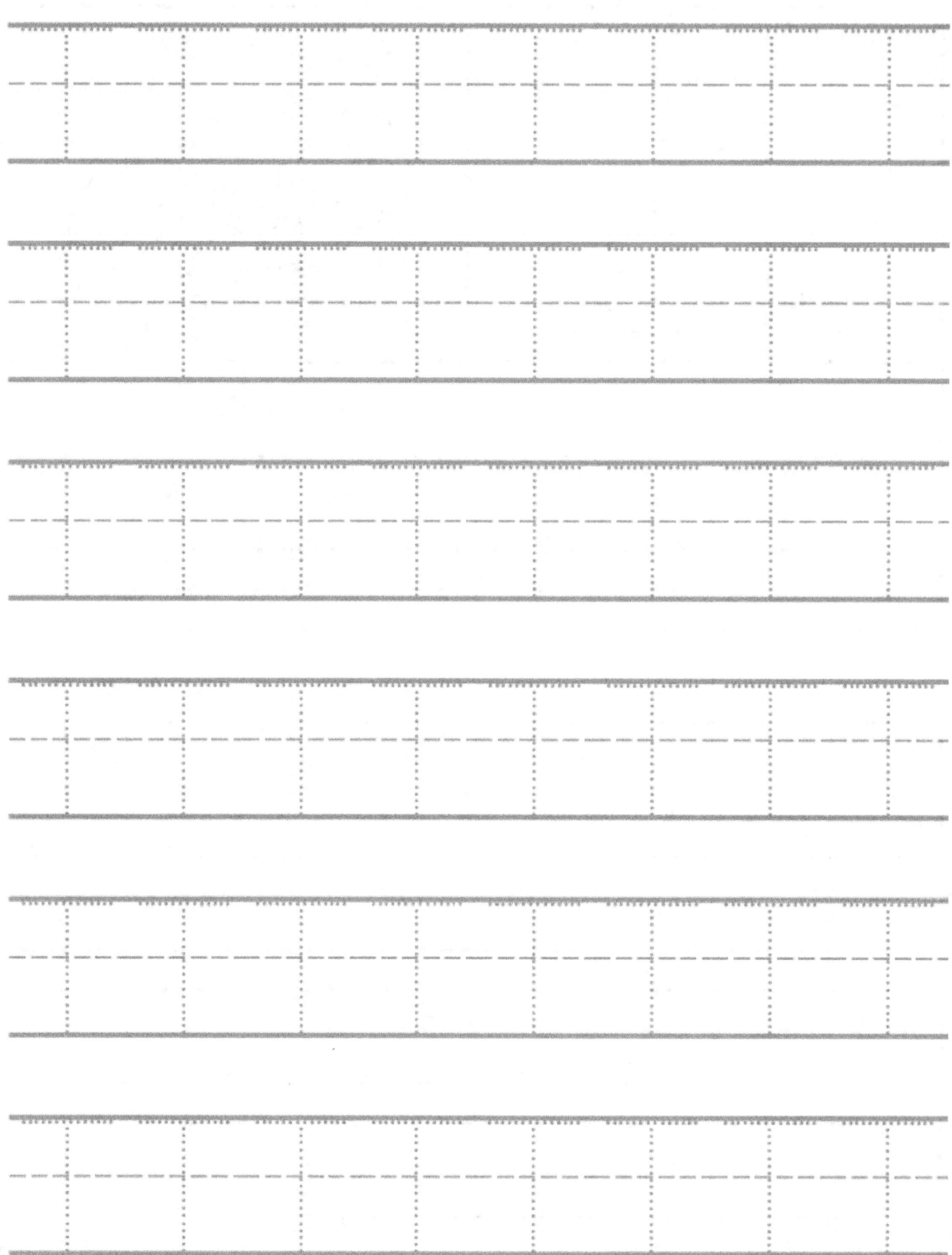

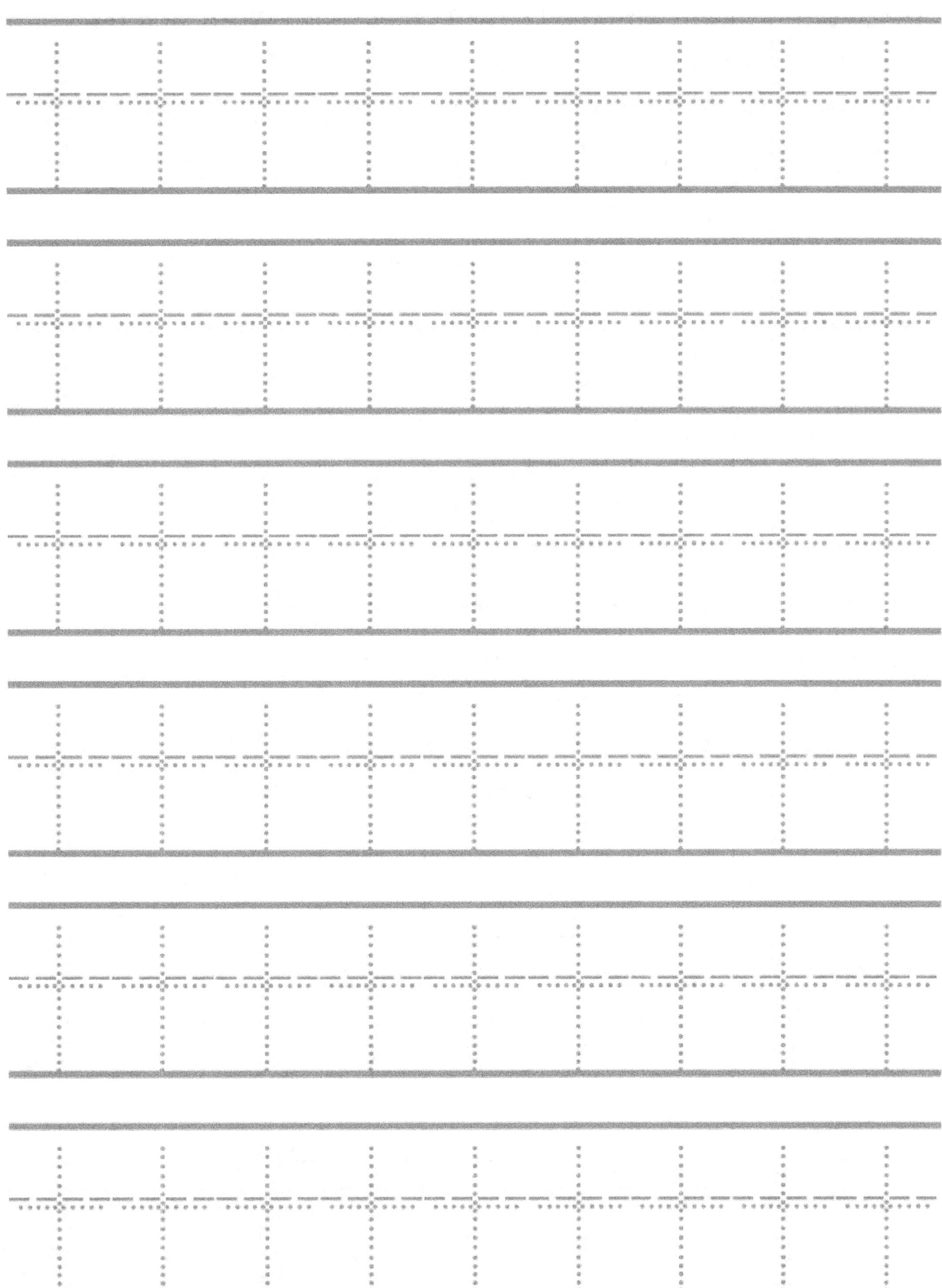

These Words begin with the Letter **T**. Trace each Word, and then print Word on the Line.

table

ten

tiger

tall

tail

taus

turtle

two

tea

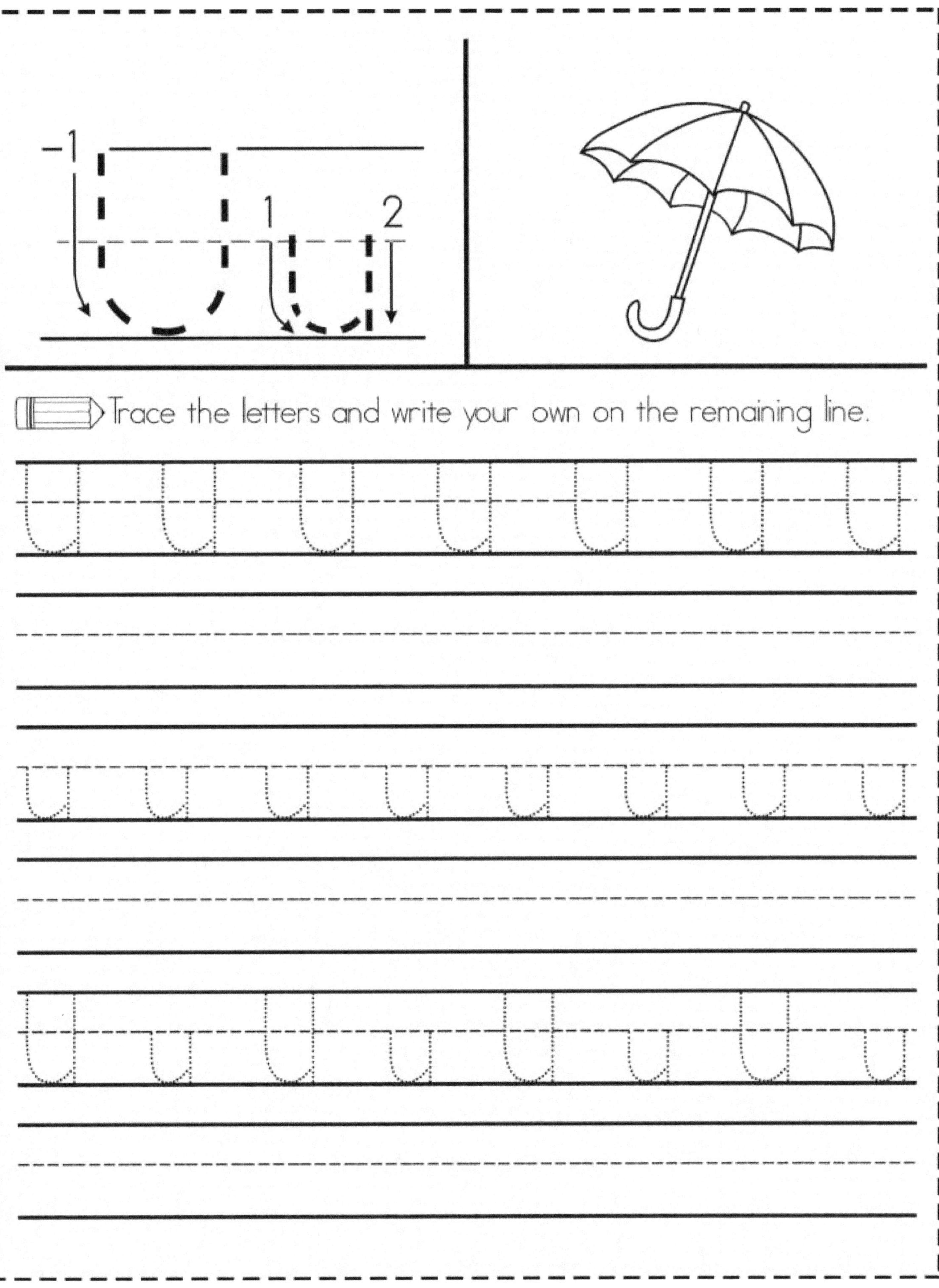



Trace the letters and write your own on the remaining line.

U U U U U U

U U U U U U

U U U U U U

U U U U U U

U U U U U U

U U U U U U

U U U U U U

These Words begin with the Letter **U**. Trace each Word, and then print Word on the Line.

uncle

under

unit

up

upper

us

use

umbrella

upon

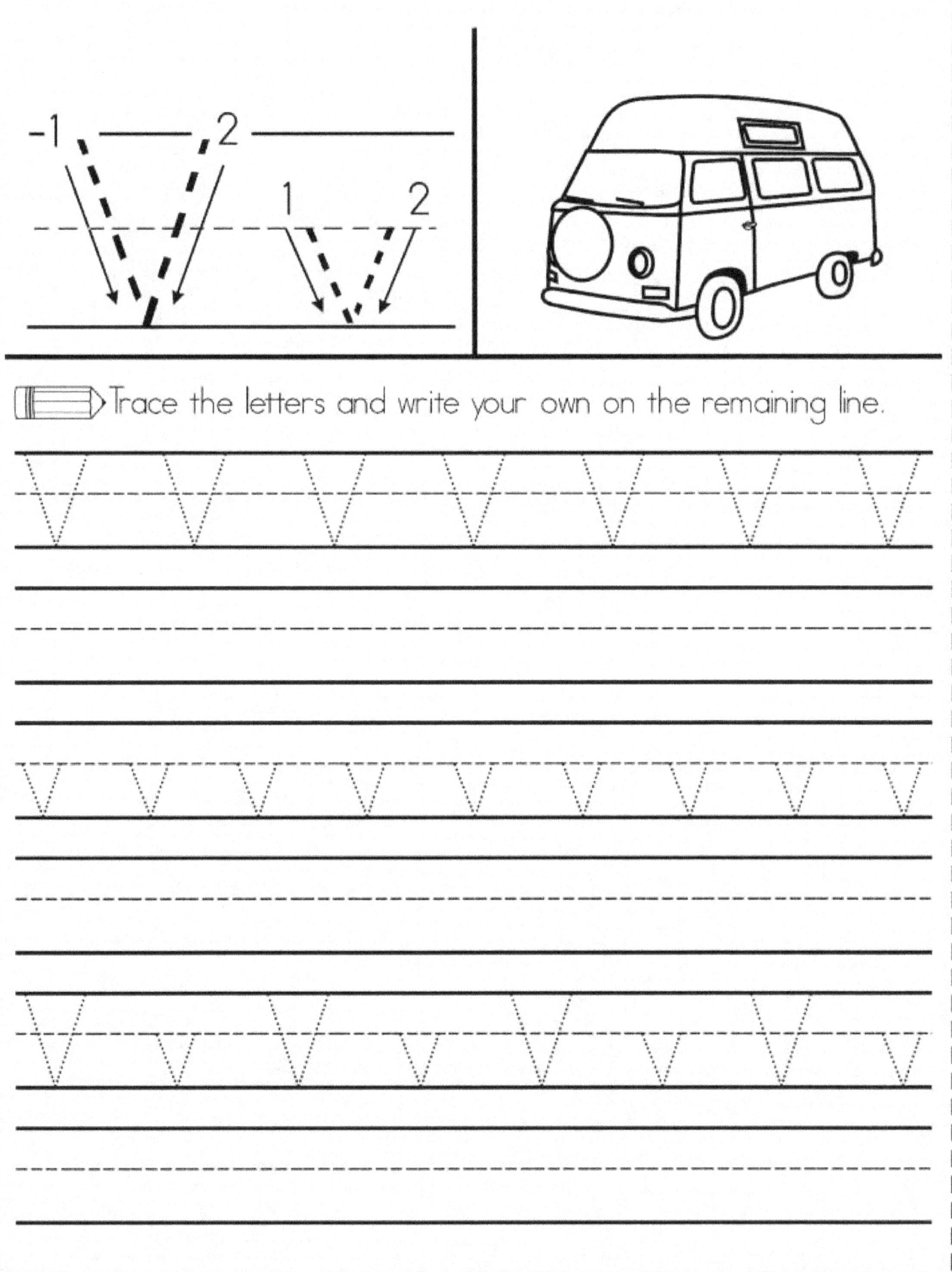

-1 2
1 2
Trace the letters and write your own on the remaining line.

These Words begin with the Letter **V**. Trace each Word, and then print Word on the Line.

van

vast

voice

view

vat

vent

very

vote

video

Trace the letters and write your own on the remaining line.

These Words begin with the Letter **W**. Trace each Word, and then print Word on the Line.

wag

warm

weather

win

want

water

what

wind

wrong

Trace the letters and write your own on the remaining line.

These Words begin with the Letter **X**. Trace each Word, and then print Word on the Line.

x-ray

xylophone

xmas

xystos

xylems

xiaosaurus

xavier

xenon

xenophobic

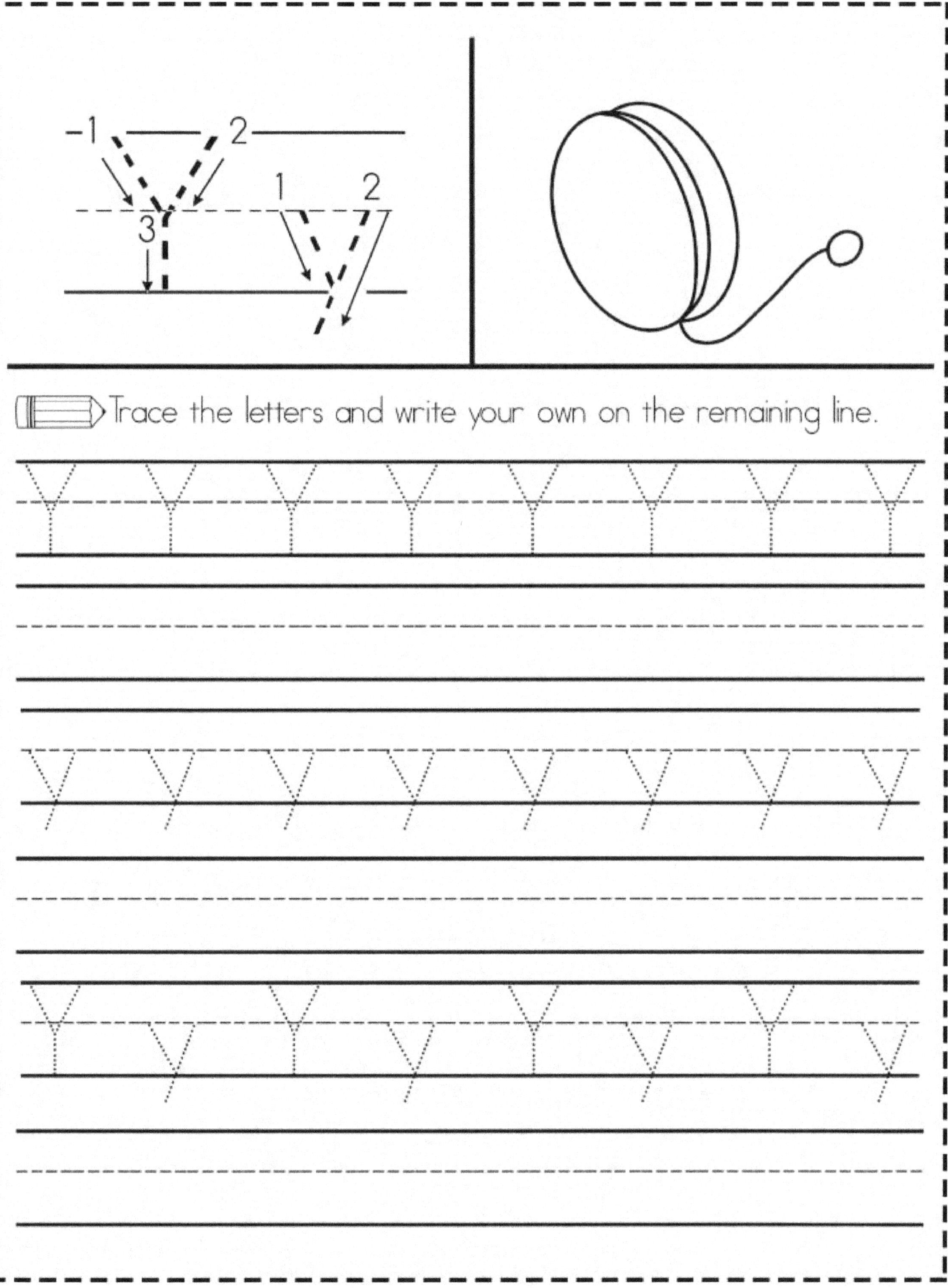

Trace the letters and write your own on the remaining line.

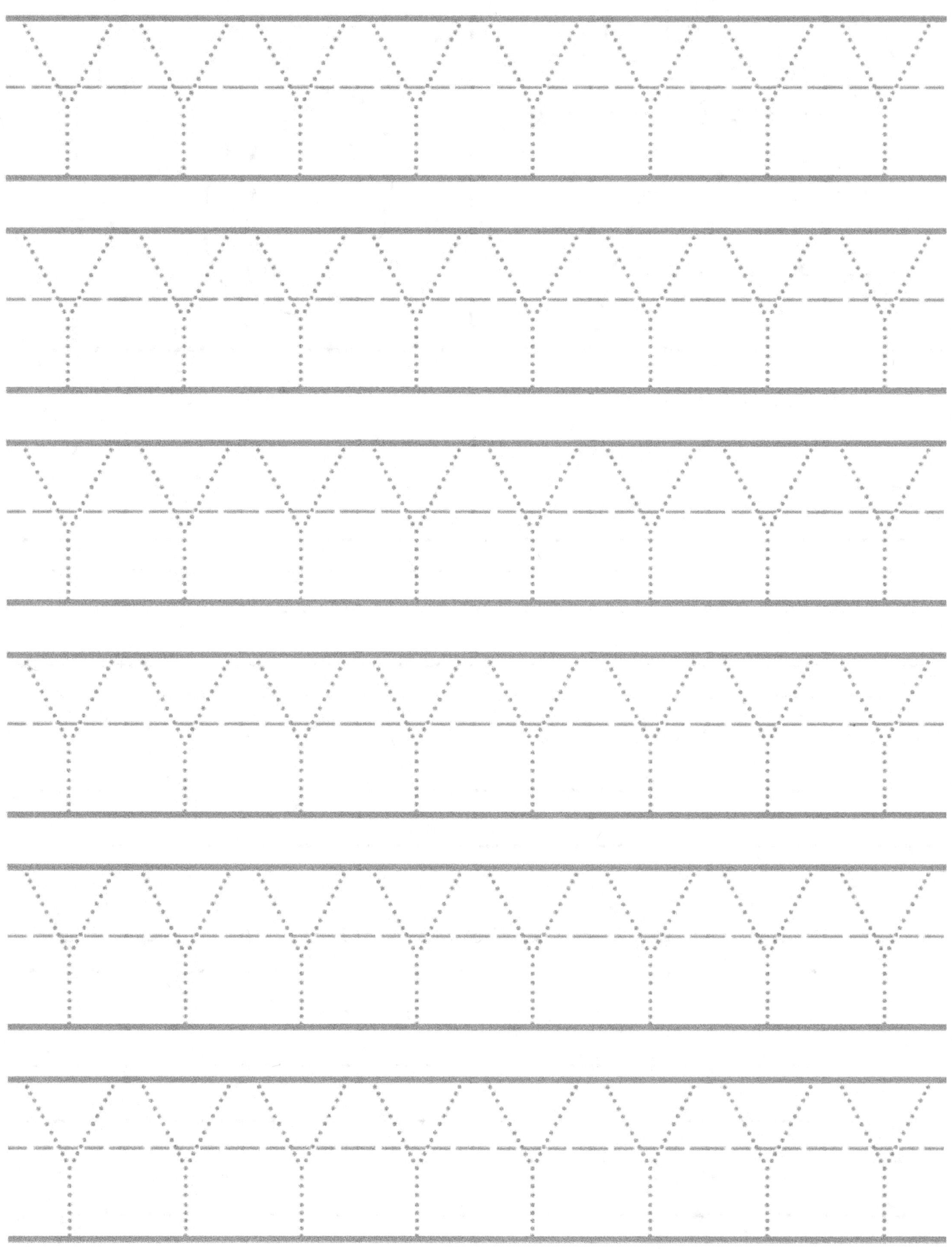

These Words begin with the Letter **Y**. Trace each Word, and then print Word on the Line.

year

yell

yellow

yes

you

your

young

yet

yummy

1
1
Trace the letters and write your own on the remaining line.

These Words begin with the Letter **Z**. Trace each Word, and then print
Word on the Line.

zoo

zip

zoom

zero

zebra

zone

zombie

zigzag

zucchini